# TEACHER'S PET PUBLICATIONS

## LITPLAN TEACHER PACK
for
### And Then There Were None
based on the novel by
Agatha Christie

Written by
Susan R. Woodward

© 2008 Teacher's Pet Publications
All Rights Reserved

Copyright Teacher's Pet Publications 2008

Only the student materials in this unit plan (such as worksheets, study questions, and tests) may be reproduced multiple times for use in the purchaser's classroom.

For any additional copyright questions, contact Teacher's Pet Publications.

www.tpet.com

# TABLE OF CONTENTS – *And Then There Were None*

| | |
|---|---|
| Introduction | 7 |
| Unit Objectives | 9 |
| Reading Assignment Sheet | 10 |
| Unit Outline | 11 |
| Study Questions (Short Answer) | 15 |
| Quiz/Study Questions (Multiple Choice) | 24 |
| Pre-reading Vocabulary Worksheets | 45 |
| Lesson One (Introductory Lesson) | 67 |
| Oral Reading Evaluation Form | 70 |
| Non-fiction Assignment Sheet | 73 |
| Writing Assignment 1 | 75 |
| Writing Assignment 2 | 80 |
| Writing Evaluation Form | 76 |
| Vocabulary Review Activities | 86 |
| Extra Writing Assignments/Discussion ?s | 89 |
| Writing Assignment 3 | 94 |
| Peer Edit Form | 96 |
| Unit Review Activities | 99 |
| Unit Tests | 105 |
| Unit Resource Materials | 161 |
| Vocabulary Resource Materials | 181 |

# ABOUT THE AUTHOR

**Agatha Christie**

Born on September 15, 1890 in Torquay, England, Agatha Mary Christie became the world's leading writer of the murder mystery. She was the daughter of Frederick Alvah Miller and Clarissa Miller. Her father died when she was a young child, and Agatha was home-schooled until, at the age of sixteen, she left England to study music in Paris. Although an accomplished pianist, she suffered from terrible stage-fright which kept her from going into a career in music.

After a trip to Cairo with her mother, Agatha turned to writing and completed her first novel, *The Mysterious Affair at Styles* (1920). In it she introduced one of the world best-known detectives, Hercule Poirot. Having been influenced by the tales of Sherlock Holmes by Sir Arthur Conan Doyle, Poirot became a manifestation of Holmes while his companion, Captain Hastings, was patterned after Holmes's Dr. Watson.

In 1914, Agatha Miller married Col. Archibald Christie and the couple had one child, a daughter, Rosalind. The marriage broke up in 1926, and Agatha Christie later married Max Mallowan in 1930. Her second husband was an archeologist, so Agatha accompanied him on many of his expeditions through Iraq and Syria. These excursions through the Middle East later formed the backdrop of some of her exotic settings.

Within her lifetime, Agatha Christie published a total of 93 books (66 of them were mysteries, but she also wrote romance novels and children's books) as well as 17 plays. Her most beloved characters are two of the best known detectives in the fictional world: Hercule Poirot and Miss Marple.

For her extraordinary success, Agatha Christie was honored with the title of Dame of the British Empire in 1971. She died peacefully of natural causes on January 12, 1976.

**Major Works**
Novels:
 - The Mysterious Affair at Styles (1920)
 - The Secret Adversary (1922)
 - The Murder on the Links (1923)
 - The Man in the Brown Suit (1924)
 - The Secret of the Chimneys (1925)
 - The Murder of Roger Ackroyd (1926)
 - The Big Four (1927)
 - The Mystery of the Blue Train (1928)
 - The Seven Dials Mystery (1929)
 - The Murder at the Vicarage (1930)
 - The Sittaford Mystery (1931)
 - Peril at End House (1932)
 - Lord Edgware Dies (1933)
 - Murder on the Orient Express (1934)
 - Why Didn't They Ask Evans? (1934)
 - Death in the Clouds (1935)
 - Three-Act Tragedy (1935)
 - The A.B.C. Murders (1936)
 - Cards on the Table (1936)
 - Murder in Mesopotamia (1936)

- Death on the Nile (1937)
- Dumb Witness (1937)
- Appointment With Death (1938)
- Hercule Poirot's Christmas (1938)
- Murder is Easy (1939)
- And Then There Were None (1939)
- One, Two, Buckle My Shoe (1940)
- Sad Cypress (1940)
- Evil Under the Sun (1940)
- N or M? (1941)
- The Body in the Library (1941)
- The Moving Finger (1942)
- Murder in Retrospect (1942)
- Death Comes as the End (1944)
- Towards Zero (1944)
- Sparkling Cyanide (1945)
- The Hollow (1946)
- Taken at the Flood (1948)
- Crooked House (1949)
- A Murder is Announced (1950)
- Mrs. McGinty's Dead (1951)
- They Came to Baghdad (1951)
- They Do It With Mirrors (1952)
- A Pocket Full of Rye (1953)
- Funerals Are Fatal (1953)
- So Many Steps to Death (1954)
- Hickory Dickory Dock (1955)
- Dead Man's Folly (1956)
- 4.50 From Paddington (1957)
- Ordeal By Innocence (1958)
- Cat Among the Pigeons (1959)
- The Pale Horse (19661)
- The Mirror Crack'd (1962)
- The Clocks (1963)
- A Caribbean Mystery (1964)
- At Bertram's Hotel (1965)
- Third Girl (1966)
- Endless Night (1967)
- By the Pricking of My Thumbs (1968)
- Hallowe'en Party (1969)
- Passenger to Frankfurt (1970)
- Nemesis (1971)
- Curtain (1975)
- Sleeping Murder (1976)

Published as Mary Westmacott:
- Giants Bread (1930)
- Unfinished Portrait (1934)
- Absent in the Spring (1944)
- An Occurrence in Scottsdale (1945)
- The Rose and The Yew Tree (1948)
- A Daughter's a Daughter (1952)
- The Burden (1956)

Plays:
- Alibi (1928)
- Black Coffee (1930)
- Love From a Stranger (1936)
- Akhnaton (1937)
- Peril at End House (1940)
- Ten Little Indians (1943)
- Appointment With Death (1945)
- Murder on the Nile/Hidden Horizon (1946)
- Murder at the Vicarage (1949)
- The Hollow (1951)
- The Mousetrap (1952)
- Witness For the Prosecution (1953)
- Spider's Web (1954)
- Towards Zero (1956)
- Verdict (1958)
- The Unexpected Guest (1958)
- Go Back For Murder (1960)
- Rule of Three (1962)

# INTRODUCTION

This LitPlan has been designed to develop students' reading, writing, thinking, and language skills through exercises and activities related to *And Then There Were None*. It includes 20 lessons, supported by extra resource materials.

The **introductory lesson** introduces students to the murder mystery genre. Following the introductory activity, students are given a transition to explain how the activity relates to the novel they are about to read. Following the transition, students are given the materials they will be using during the unit. At the end of the lesson, students begin the pre-reading work for the first reading assignment.

The **reading assignments** are approximately thirty pages each; some are a little shorter while others are a little longer. Students have approximately 15 minutes of pre-reading work to do prior to each reading assignment. This pre-reading work involves reviewing the study questions for the assignment and doing some vocabulary work for 10 vocabulary words they will encounter in their reading.

The **study guide questions** are fact-based questions; students can find the answers to these questions right in the text. These questions come in two formats: short answer or multiple choice. The best use of these materials is probably to use the short answer version of the questions as study guides for students (since answers will be more complete), and to use the multiple choice version for occasional quizzes.

The **vocabulary work** is intended to enrich students' vocabularies as well as to aid in the students' understanding of the novel. Prior to each reading assignment, students will complete a two-part worksheet for 10 vocabulary words in the upcoming reading assignment. Part I focuses on students' use of general knowledge and contextual clues by giving the sentence in which the word appears in the text. Students are then to write down what they think the words mean based on the words' usage. Part II nails down the definitions of the words by giving students dictionary definitions of the words and having students match the words to the correct definitions based on the words' contextual usage. Students should then have an understanding of the words when they meet them in the text.

After each reading assignment, students will go back and formulate answers for the study guide questions. Discussion of these questions serves as a **review** of the most important events and ideas presented in the reading assignments.

After students complete reading the work, there is a **vocabulary review** lesson which pulls together all of the fragmented vocabulary lists for the reading assignments and gives students a review of all of the words they have studied.

Following the vocabulary review, a lesson is devoted to the **extra discussion questions/writing assignments**. These questions focus on interpretation, critical analysis, and personal response, employing a variety of thinking skills and adding to the students' understanding of the novel.

There are three **writing assignments** in this unit, each with the purpose of informing, persuading, or having students express personal opinions.
1. writing a mystery story based on a factual unsolved mystery (personal response)
2. researching topics related to a character from *And Then There Were None* (informative)
3. corporal punishment (persuasive)

There is a **non-fiction reading assignment**. Students must read non-fiction articles, books, etc. to gather information about topics related to the novel.

The **review lesson** pulls together all of the aspects of the unit. The teacher is given four or five choices of activities or games to use which all serve the same basic function of reviewing all of the information presented in the unit.

The **unit test** comes in two formats: multiple choice or short answer. As a convenience, two different tests for each format have been included. There is also an advanced short answer unit test for advanced students.

There are additional **support materials** included with this unit. The **Unit Resource Materials** section includes suggestions for an in-class library, crossword and word search puzzles related to the novel, and extra worksheets. There is a list of **bulletin board ideas** which gives the teacher suggestions for bulletin boards to go along with this unit. In addition, there is a list of **extra class activities** the teacher could choose from to enhance the unit or as a substitution for an exercise the teacher might feel is inappropriate for his/her class. **Answer keys** are located directly after the **reproducible student materials** throughout the unit. The **Vocabulary Resource Materials** section includes similar worksheets and games to reinforce the vocabulary words.

The **level** of this unit can be varied depending upon the criteria on which the individual assignments are graded, the teacher's expectations of his/her students in class discussions, and the formats chosen for the study guides, quizzes and test. If teachers have other ideas/activities they wish to use, they can usually easily be inserted prior to the review lesson.

The student materials may be reproduced for use in the teacher's classroom without infringement of copyrights. No other portion of this unit may be reproduced without the written consent of Teacher's Pet Publications, Inc.

# UNIT OBJECTIVES *And Then There Were None*

1. Through reading Agatha Christie's *And Then There Were None*, students will learn about the history of the mystery genre and about the woman who has become the world's leading mystery writer.

2. Students will demonstrate their understanding of the text on four levels: factual, interpretive, critical, and personal.

3. Students will create board games based on the novel.

4. Students will be given the opportunity to practice reading aloud and silently to improve their skills in each area.

5. Students will answer questions to demonstrate their knowledge and understanding of the main events and characters in *And Then There Were None* as they relate to the author's theme development: the effect of guilt on the conscience, crime and punishment, corporal punishment, and taking the law into one's own hands.

6. Students will enrich their vocabularies and improve their understanding of the novel through the vocabulary lessons prepared for use in conjunction with the novel.

7. The writing assignments in this unit are geared to several purposes:

    a. To have students demonstrate their abilities to inform, to persuade, or to express their own personal ideas
       Note: Students will demonstrate the ability to write effectively to inform by developing and organizing facts to convey information. Students will demonstrate the ability to write effectively to persuade by selecting and organizing relevant information, establishing an argumentative purpose, and by designing an appropriate strategy for an identified audience. Students will demonstrate the ability to write effectively to express personal ideas by selecting a form and appropriate elements.

    b. To check the students' reading comprehension

    c. To make students think about the ideas presented by the novel

    d. To encourage logical thinking

    e. To provide an opportunity to practice good grammar and improve students' use of the English language.

8. Students will read aloud, report, and participate in large and small group discussions to improve their public speaking and personal interaction skills.

READING ASSIGNMENTS *And Then There Were None*

| Date Assigned | Assignment | Completion Date |
|---|---|---|
| | *Assignment 1*<br>Chapters 1-2 | |
| | *Assignment 2*<br>Chapters 3-4 | |
| | *Assignment 3*<br>Chapters 5-6 | |
| | *Assignment 4*<br>Chapters 7-8 | |
| | *Assignment 5*<br>Chapters 9-10 | |
| | *Assignment 6*<br>Chapters 11-12 | |
| | *Assignment 7*<br>Chapters 13-14 | |
| | *Assignment 8*<br>Chapters 15-16 | |
| | *Assignment 9*<br>Epilogue and Letter | |

## UNIT OUTLINE *And Then There Were None*

| 1 | 2 | 3 | 4 | 5 |
|---|---|---|---|---|
| Intro the mystery genre: "Murders in the Rue Morgue" PVR Ch. 1-2 | Study ?s Ch. 1-2 Oral Reading PVR Ch. 3-4 | Study ?s Ch. 3-4 Non-fiction Assignment: Media Center for research PVR Ch. 5-6 | Study ?s Ch. 5-6 Non-fiction findings Writing Assignment #1 PVR Ch. 7-8 | Study ?s Ch. 7-8 Character sketch posters PVR Ch. 9-10 |
| 6 | 7 | 8 | 9 | 10 |
| Study ?s Ch. 9-10 Oral Reading PVR Ch. 11-12 | Study ?s Ch. 11-12 Writing Assignment #2: Media Center for research PVR Ch. 13-14 | Study ?s Ch. 13-14 Assign group project: board games PVR Ch. 15-16 | Study ?s Ch. 15-16 Oral Reading PVR Epilogue and Letter | Study ?s Epilogue and Letter Work on Writing Assignment #1 |
| 11 | 12 | 13 | 14 | 15 |
| Group Work: Game Project | Vocabulary Review | Extra Discussion Questions | Game Day: play student created board games | Writing Assignment #3 In-Class Writing: Persuasive |
| 16 | 17 | 18 | 19 | 20 |
| Peer Editing: Persuasive Piece | Presentations Day 1: Story-telling | Presentations Day 2: Story-telling | Unit Review | Unit Test |

Key: P = Preview Study Questions   V – Vocabulary Work   R = Read

# STUDY GUIDE QUESTIONS

# STUDY GUIDE QUESTIONS *And Then There Were None*

**Assignment 1**
Chapters 1-2
1. What are the rumors surrounding Indian Island?
2. Why is Vera Claythorne going to Indian Island?
3. What seems to be Dr. Armstrong's "specialty"?
4. What warning does Blore receive from the old man on the train?
5. How does Lombard avoid answering Vera Claythorne's questions about the Owens?
6. Who is Mr. Davis?
7. Describe Anthony Marston.
8. Who is the captain of the passenger boat?

**Assignment 2**
Chapters 3-4
1. What is in the center of the dining room table?
2. What hangs above the mantelpiece in each of the bedrooms in the island mansion?
3. The guests arrive, get situated, and have a nice dinner. What happens after dinner?
4. What is the title of the record that Rogers played?
5. What reason does Emily Brent give for coming to Indian Island?
6. Of what crime does the "voice" accuse each person in the house?
7. What conclusion does Wargrave come to about the owner of the house?
8. What accusation is made against Wargrave?
9. What had happened to Dr. Armstrong's patient?
10. Who is the one person who refuses to speak about the charges made against him/her?
11. What happens to Anthony Marston?

**Assignment 3**
Chapters 5-6
1. Upon what does Judge Wargrave reflect about the Seton case?
2. What discovery does Rogers make when he goes to clear the dinner dishes from the dining room?
3. How did Arthur Richmond die?
4. Who was Hugo?
5. What news does Rogers bring to Dr. Armstrong?
6. What are the guests anxious about their first morning on the island?
7. What news does Armstrong break to the group immediately following breakfast?
8. What conclusion does General Macarthur make about their being lured to the island?
9. What has Rogers particularly upset at the end of Chapter 6?

**Assignment 4**
Chapters 7-8
1. What does Emily Brent suspect about Mr. and Mrs. Rogers?
2. Who was Beatrice Taylor?
3. How does Armstrong suspect that the Rogers' killed their employer?
4. Why doesn't Lombard believe that Mrs. Rogers killed herself?
5. What do Lombard and Armstrong conclude about the nursery rhyme?
6. After their search, what do Blore, Armstrong, and Lombard discover about the island?
7. Which of the characters has accepted his/her fate and waits patiently for the final outcome?
8. How has Emily Brent decided to pass the time?
9. What is the sound that Blore, Armstrong, and Lombard hear from upstairs?
10. After searching the entire house, what do Armstrong, Blore, and Lombard conclude?

**Assignment 5**
Chapters 9-10
1. What suggestion does Blore make about Mrs. Rogers's death?
2. What is it that Blore demands to know from Lombard?
3. What does Lombard confess actually brought him to Indian Island?
4. What observation does Vera make about the weather?
5. How does Macarthur die?
6. What did Vera and Rogers discover in the dining room right after General Macarthur is found on the beach?
7. What conclusion does Judge Wargrave come to concerning Mr. Owen?
8. Whose name does Emily Brent write in her diary as the murderer?
9. What item does Rogers claim is missing that has him nervous and upset?
10. What does Rogers do to prevent the disappearance of any more Indian figurines?

**Assignment 6**
Chapters 11-12
1. What news does Lombard share with Blore when he awakens him in the morning?
2. What happens to Rogers?
3. Why does Vera begin to laugh uncontrollably?
4. What does Blore confess to Lombard?
5. Emily Brent dreams of Beatrice Taylor. What is Beatrice doing in the dream?
6. While clearing breakfast dishes Emily Brent feels a little giddy, she sits to wait for the feeling to pass. What does she see on the windowpane?
7. How is Emily Brent murdered?
8. Who immediately falls under suspicion for Emily's murder?
9. What does Mr. Lombard find missing from his bed-table?
10. Where are the potentially lethal drugs put for safekeeping?

**Assignment 7**
Chapters 13-14
1. Who are the five remaining guests on Indian island?
2. Which of the characters is said to look like "a wary old tortoise"?
3. Vera goes to her room to bathe her aching head and temples in cold water. What causes her screams of terror?
4. When Mr. Justice Wargrave is discovered dead what is strange about his appearance?
5. What meals are the survivors reduced to eating?
6. Who finds the revolver?
7. What does Vera see in her room that she had not noticed before?
8. Who hears someone sneaking around the house and decides to investigate?
9. Who disappears at the end of Chapter 14?

**Assignment 8**
Chapters 15-16
1. What change has occurred in the weather at the opening of Chapter 15?
2. How does Lombard suggest the survivors make contact with people on the mainland?
3. What does Vera suddenly remember about the nursery rhyme that makes the party think that Dr. Armstrong is still alive?
4. What happens to Blore?
5. What do Vera and Lombard find that ends up pitting them against each other?
6. When staring at him on the beach, to what does Vera compare Lombard's face?
7. What does Vera do when she and Lombard are dragging Dr. Armstrong's body away from the sea?
8. What happens to Philip Lombard?
9. Who does Vera believe is waiting for her in her bedroom?
10. How does Vera Claythorne die?

**Assignment 9**
Epilogue and Letter
1. What does the Assistant Commissioner of Scotland Yard find on Indian Island?
2. Identify Isaac Morris.
3. Why had the people of Sticklehaven not attempted to make contact with anyone on Indian Island?
4. Why did Fred Narracott ignore the edict regarding Indian Island and take his boat over there?
5. What makes the inspector absolutely certain that Vera Claythorne had not committed the murders?
6. How do the police manage to solve the crime of Indian Island?
7. Who was the murderer on Indian Island?
8. Why did the murderer decide on these particular ten victims?
9. Which of the killer's victims did not actually die on Indian Island?
10. How did the killer manage to complete the scheme without getting caught by the others?

# STUDY GUIDE QUESTIONS ANSWER KEY *And Then There Were None*

## Chapters 1-2

1. What are the rumors surrounding Indian Island?
   *An American millionaire who loved sailing purchased the island only to turn around and sell it because his third wife was a bad sailor. It is also rumored to have been purchased by a Mr. Owen, a Hollywood film star, and a member of the royal family. The island was also rumored to be used for secret military operations.*

2. Why is Vera Claythorne going to Indian Island?
   *She has been hired to be a temporary secretary to Mrs. Una Nancy Owen.*

3. What seems to be Dr. Armstrong's "specialty"?
   *He cons rich women with fake diagnoses and treatments for imagined illnesses.*

4. What warning does Blore receive from the old man on the train?
   *The old man tells him that the day of judgment is very close at hand.*

5. How does Lombard avoid answering Vera Claythorne's questions about the Owens?
   *He distracts her by telling her there is a wasp on her arm and pretends to swat it.*

6. Who is Mr. Davis?
   *Mr. Davis is the fake name assumed by Mr. Blore. He works for Mr. Owen.*

7. Describe Anthony Marston.
   *He is a young handsome man who "looks, not a man, but a young God, a Hero God out of some Northern Saga."*

8. Who is the captain of the passenger boat?
   *Fred Narracott owns the boat and takes the passengers to Indian Island.*

## Chapters 3-4

1. What is in the center of the dining room table?
   *Ten china figures of little Indian boys are set in a circle in the center of the dining room table.*

2. What hangs above the mantelpiece in each of the bedrooms in the island mansion?
   *A framed verse, "The Little Indian Boys," hangs over the mantelpieces of each bedroom in the island mansion.*

3. The guests arrive, get situated, and have a nice dinner. What happens after dinner?
   *A mysterious voice, seeming to come from nowhere, makes accusations about each of the guests.*

4. What is the title of the record that Rogers played?
   *The record is titled "Swan Song."*

5. What reason does Emily Brent give for coming to Indian Island?
   *She received an invitation to join a friend she'd met two summers ago for a holiday at Indian Island.*

6. Of what crime does the "voice" accuse each person in the house?
   *Each of the guests are accused of murder.*

7. What conclusion does Wargrave come to about the owner of the house?
   *Both the initials of the owner and his wife were U. N. with the last name Owen. Wargrave concludes that U.N. Owen is an unknown person who has lured them all to the island.*

8. What accusation is made against Wargrave?
   *Wargrave is charged with sentencing an innocent man, Edward Seton, to death.*

9. What had happened to Dr. Armstrong's patient?
   *The woman died on the operating table because he was drunk when performing surgery.*
10. Who is the one person who refuses to speak about the charges made against him/her?
    *Emily Brent refuses to speak about the charges made against her.*
11. What happens to Anthony Marston?
    *He suddenly collapses after taking a drink from his glass.*

## Chapters 5-6

1. Upon what does Judge Wargrave reflect about the Seton case?
   *He remembers that he had "cooked Seton's goose."*
2. What discovery does Rogers make when he goes to clear the dinner dishes from the dining room?
   *Rogers notices that one of the little Indian boy figurines is missing.*
3. How did Arthur Richmond die?
   *General Macarthur had sent him on a reconnaissance mission where Richmond was killed.*
4. Who was Hugo?
   *Hugo was the handsome uncle of Vera Claythorne's ward, Cyril.*
5. What news does Rogers bring to Dr. Armstrong?
   *Rogers tells Dr. Armstrong that he can not wake his wife.*
6. What are the guests anxious about their first morning on the island?
   *They are anxiously awaiting the arrival of Fred Narracott and the boat.*
7. What news does Armstrong break to the group immediately following breakfast?
   *Dr. Armstrong tells the group that Mrs. Rogers is dead.*
8. What conclusion does General Macarthur make about their being lured to the island?
   *General Macarthur is sure they will never leave the island.*
9. What has Rogers particularly upset at the end of Chapter 6?
   *Rogers notices that there are now only eight figurines on the dining room table.*

## Chapters 7-8

1. What does Emily Brent suspect about Mr. and Mrs. Rogers?
   *Emily suspects that the story of them killing their employer for the legacy is true.*
2. Who was Beatrice Taylor?
   *She was Emily Brent's servant who killed herself after Emily fired her from her job when the girl discovered she was pregnant.*
3. How does Armstrong suspect that the Rogers' killed their employer?
   *Dr. Armstrong suspects they withheld the old woman's medication that she needed to live.*
4. Why doesn't Lombard believe that Mrs. Rogers killed herself?
   *Lombard believes that it is too much of a coincidence for two suicides to occur within such a short time period.*
5. What do Lombard and Armstrong conclude about the nursery rhyme?
   *They conclude the murderer must be hiding on the island and killing off the guests in the order outlined in the nursery rhyme.*
6. After their search, what do Blore, Armstrong, and Lombard discover about the island?
   *They discover there is no place to hide on the island except for inside the house.*

7. Which of the characters has accepted his/her fate and waits patiently for the final outcome?
   *General Macarthur has admitted his guilt and accepts his fate.*

8. How has Emily Brent decided to pass the time?
   *She sits on the terrace, knitting.*

9. What is the sound that Blore, Armstrong, and Lombard hear from upstairs?
   *The noises from upstairs are Rogers packing his belongings and preparing to move into one of the empty guest rooms. He does not want to be in a room with his wife's dead body.*

10. After searching the entire house, what do Armstrong, Blore, and Lombard conclude?
    *They conclude there is no one on the island except for the eight remaining guests.*

**Chapters 9-10**

1. What suggestion does Blore make about Mrs. Rogers's death?
   *Blore accuses Dr. Armstrong of making a mistake and giving her an overdose of the sedative.*

2. What is it that Blore demands to know from Lombard?
   *Blore wants to know why Lombard felt it necessary to bring a revolver to what was supposed to be a social event.*

3. What does Lombard confess actually brought him to Indian Island?
   *He was paid one hundred guineas by Mr. Morris to come to the island and "keep his eyes open."*

4. What observation does Vera make about the weather?
   *She notices that a terrible storm is coming.*

5. How does Macarthur die?
   *General Macarthur is found bludgeoned to death on the beach.*

6. What did Vera and Rogers discover in the dining room right after General Macarthur is found on the beach?
   *Vera and Rogers find only seven Indian figurines are left.*

7. What conclusion does Judge Wargrave come to concerning Mr. Owen?
   *Judge Wargrave concludes that Mr. Owen must be one of the members of the group.*

8. Whose name does Emily Brent write in her diary as the murderer?
   *She unconsciously writes Beatrice Taylor's name as the murderer.*

9. What item does Rogers claim is missing that has him nervous and upset?
   *Rogers is upset to find that a scarlet oilsilk curtain is missing from the bathroom.*

10. What does Rogers do to prevent the disappearance of any more Indian figurines?
    *He locks the door to the dining room and pockets the key so that no more figurines can disappear.*

**Chapters 11-12**

1. What news does Lombard share with Blore when he awakens him in the morning?
   *Blore claims that Rogers is missing.*

2. What happens to Rogers?
   *He is killed with an axe while chopping wood.*

3. Why does Vera begin to laugh uncontrollably?
   *She realizes that the deaths are following the rhyme, but there are no bees on the island for the next death to take place.*
4. What does Blore confess to Lombard?
   *He admits to committing perjury causing an innocent man to go to prison where the man later dies.*
5. Emily Brent dreams of Beatrice Taylor. What is Beatrice doing in the dream?
   *Beatrice is outside pressing her face against the window and moaning, asking to be let in.*
6. While clearing breakfast dishes Emily Brent feels a little giddy, she sits to wait for the feeling to pass. What does she see on the windowpane?
   *She sees a bee crawling up the windowpane.*
7. How is Emily Brent murdered?
   *Emily is injected in the neck with poison.*
8. Who immediately falls under suspicion for Emily's murder?
   *Dr. Armstrong is immediately suspected of murdering Emily.*
9. What does Mr. Lombard find missing from his bed-table?
   *His revolver is missing.*
10. Where are the potentially lethal drugs put for safekeeping?
    *The drugs are put into a locked chest (Blore holds this key) and the locked chest is locked in the pantry (Lombard holds this key).*

## Chapters 13-14

1. Who are the five remaining guests on Indian island?
   *The five remaining guests are Mr. Justice Wargrave, Ex-Inspector Blore, Philip Lombard, Vera Claythorne, and Dr. Armstrong.*
2. Which of the characters is said to look like "a wary old tortoise"?
   *Judge Wargrave is said to look like "a wary old tortoise."*
3. Vera goes to her room to bathe her aching head and temples in cold water. What causes her screams of terror?
   *Someone has hung seaweed from a hook on the ceiling of her room, and she walks into it thinking the seaweed is a cold, damp hand.*
4. When Mr. Justice Wargrave is discovered dead what is strange about his appearance?
   *Judge Wargrave is found dressed as a judge with a grey wig (Emily's missing yarn) and a scarlet "robe" (the missing oilsilk). He'd been shot through the head.*
5. What meals are the survivors reduced to eating?
   *The survivors are reduced to eating cold tongue from a tin while standing around a table in the kitchen.*
6. Who finds the revolver?
   *Philip Lombard finds the revolver in the drawer of his bedside table.*
7. What does Vera see in her room that she had not noticed before?
   *She sees a large hook in the ceiling near her bed.*
8. Who hears someone sneaking around the house and decides to investigate?
   *Blore hears noises and decides to find out who is sneaking around in the dark.*
9. Who disappears at the end of Chapter 14?
   *Dr. Armstrong disappears.*

**Chapters 15-16**
1. What change has occurred in the weather at the opening of Chapter 15?
   *The sun is shining and the storm is over.*
2. How does Lombard suggest the survivors make contact with people on the mainland?
   *He is going to use a mirror to heliograph an S O S to the mainland.*
3. What does Vera suddenly remember about the nursery rhyme that makes the party think that Dr. Armstrong is still alive?
   *She remembers the line about the red herring in the nursery rhyme, so she believes that Armstrong is trying to trick them by taking the figurine to make them believe he is dead.*
4. What happens to Blore?
   *His skull is crushed by a marble clock that is in the shape of a bear.*
5. What do Vera and Lombard find that ends up pitting them against each other?
   *They find Armstrong's drowned body lying on the beach and he has been dead for some time.*
6. When staring at him on the beach, to what does Vera compare Lombard's face?
   *She thinks he looks like a wolf with jagged teeth.*
7. What does Vera do when she and Lombard are dragging Dr. Armstrong's body away from the sea?
   *She takes the revolver from Lombard's pocket.*
8. What happens to Philip Lombard?
   *Philip Lombard is shot by Vera Claythorne.*
9. Who does Vera believe is waiting for her in her bedroom?
   *She thinks Hugo is waiting for her in her bedroom.*
10. How does Vera Claythorne die?
    *Vera hangs herself.*

**Epilogue and Letter**
1. What does the Assistant Commissioner of Scotland Yard find on Indian Island?
   *He finds ten dead bodies and not a living soul on the island.*
2. Identify Isaac Morris.
   *He had made all the arrangements for the purchase of the island for an unnamed third party.*
3. Why had the people of Sticklehaven not attempted to make contact with anyone on Indian Island?
   *Mr. Morris had told the townsfolk that Mr. Owen was hosting a contest about who could best survive on a desert island for a week and that no one from the town could interfere.*
4. Why did Fred Narracott ignore the edict regarding Indian Island and take his boat over there?
   *He thought that the guests of the island seemed too normal to be involved in anything like Robson's parties, and the S O S made him suspicious.*
5. What makes the inspector absolutely certain that Vera Claythorne had not committed the murders?
   *Although she hanged herself, the chair she had stood on was placed neatly back by the wall by someone else after her death.*
6. How do the police manage to solve the crime of Indian Island?
   *A fisherman finds a confession in a sealed bottle floating in the water.*

7. Who was the murderer on Indian Island?
   *The murderer was Judge Lawrence Wargrave.*

8. Why did the murderer decide on these particular ten victims?
   *All were guilty of murder, yet the law could not touch them.*

9. Which of the killer's victims did not actually die on Indian Island?
   *Judge Wargrave did not want to leave any loose ends, so he gave Isaac Morris some medicine to offset his indigestion; it was poison.*

10. How did the killer manage to complete the scheme without getting caught by the others?
    *Wargrave faked his death with the help of Dr. Armstrong. He got him to go along with it by telling the doctor that he could watch over the group and ferret out the killer if everyone thought he was dead. Wargrave later pushed his accomplice off a cliff.*

MULTIPLE CHOICE STUDY/QUIZ QUESTIONS
*And Then There Were None*

**Assignment 1**
**Chapters 1-2**

1. Which is NOT one of the rumors surrounding Indian Island?
    A. A famous Hollywood actress bought the island.
    B. An American millionaire owned the place, but sold it because his third wife didn't sail.
    C. The island was being used for top secret military operations.
    D. The Queen of England planned to use it as a holiday retreat.

2. Why is Vera Claythorne going to Indian Island?
    A. She is to serve as temporary secretary to Mrs. Owen.
    B. She is meeting old friends for a holiday.
    C. She is the new cook for Mrs. Owen.
    D. She is getting married on the island.

3. What seems to be Dr. Armstrong's "specialty"?
    A. He performs illegal abortions.
    B. He assists terminally ill patients commit suicide.
    C. He cons rich women with fake diagnoses to imagined illnesses.
    D. He is a plastic surgeon.

4. What warning does Blore receive from the old man on the train?
    A. The old man tells him that the day of judgment is very close at hand.
    B. The old man tells Blore that someone is out to kill him.
    C. The old man tells him to stay away from Indian Island.
    D. He'd better be properly dressed for the upcoming storm.

5. How does Lombard avoid answering Vera Claythorne's questions about the Owens?
    A. He suddenly kisses her.
    B. He drops his coffee cup, spilling some of its contents on her.
    C. He pretends that a wasp is crawling up her arm and swats at it.
    D. He pretends to know one of the other passengers on the boat and waves at him.

6. Who is Mr. Davis?
    A. He is the real owner of Indian Island.
    B. He is a doctor who has been invited on holiday at Indian Island.
    C. He is the owner of the boat that will take the group to Indian Island.
    D. It is Mr. Blore's fake name.

7. Describe Anthony Marston.
    A. He is a middle-aged lawyer with small spectacles and bushy eyebrows.
    B. He is a retired general in the British army.
    C. He is an old man who looks like a turtle with his head pulled into his neck.
    D. He is a young man who is compared to a God.

8. Who is the captain of the passenger boat?
    A. Anthony Marston
    B. Fred Narracott
    C. Lawrence Wargrave
    D. Davis Blore

**Assignment 2**
**Chapters 3-4**

1. What is in the center of the dining room table?
    A. A large bouquet of flowers
    B. Tea service for ten
    C. Ten china figurines of Indian boys
    D. A bowl of apples

2. What hangs above the mantelpiece in each of the bedrooms in the island mansion?
    A. A framed nursery rhyme
    B. A gruesome picture of Mr. U.N. Owen
    C. A seascape
    D. A map of the island

3. The guests arrive, get situated, and have a nice dinner. What happens after dinner?
    A. Mr. Owen finally arrives, fashionably late.
    B. A mysterious voice from an unknown source makes accusations about each of the guests.
    C. There is a huge storm, and the lights go out.
    D. A woman screams, a shot rings out, and the guests hear a loud "thud" from the floor above.

4. What is the title of the record that Rogers played?
    A. Who Wants to Live Forever
    B. I Shot the Sheriff
    C. Till Death Do Us Part
    D. Swan Song

5. What reason does Emily Brent give for coming to Indian Island?
    A. One of her former students had recommended the Island as a wonderful vacation spot.
    B. Her doctor told her that a vacation by the sea would be good for her poor health.
    C. She is hired as the new cook on Indian Island.
    D. She said she is meeting an old friend who had invited her for a holiday.

6. Of what crime does the "voice" accuse each person in the house?
    A. Murder
    B. Adultery
    C. Arson
    D. Extortion

7. What conclusion does Wargrave come to about the owner of the house?
   A. He will be arriving late to confront them face-to-face.
   B. He is a rich man pulling a publicity stunt.
   C. The owner of the house is really Rogers using a phony name.
   D. Because of his initials "U. N." and last name "Owen," he must be "unknown" to them.

8. What accusation is made against Wargrave?
   A. He killed his employer for a legacy left in her will.
   B. He ran over some children while speeding in his car.
   C. He sentenced an innocent man to death.
   D. He killed his wife in a jealous rage.

9. What had happened to Dr. Armstrong's patient?
   A. He permanently scarred the beautiful woman's face out of jealousy.
   B. She died on the operating table because he was drunk during surgery.
   C. She killed herself after he blackmailed her into sleeping with him.
   D. She died after he used cheap implants that disintegrated, putting silicone in her system.

10. Who is the one person who refuses to speak about the charges made against him/her?
    A. Anthony Marston
    B. Mrs. Rogers
    C. Emily Brent
    D. Vera Claythorne

11. What happens to Anthony Marston?
    A. He makes a pass at Vera Claythorne, and she slaps him.
    B. He suddenly collapses after taking a drink from his glass.
    C. He shoots himself through the head out of a sense of remorse.
    D. He storms out of the house and takes off in the only boat.

**Assignment 3**
**Chapters 5-6**

1. Upon what does Judge Wargrave reflect about the Seton case?
    A. He remembers how the defense attorney was so incompetent.
    B. He reflects on how he knew Seton was innocent and took pleasure in sentencing him.
    C. He remembers how beautiful the prosecuting attorney was.
    D. He remembers that "he'd cooked Seton's goose."

2. What discovery does Rogers make when he goes to clear the dinner dishes from the dining room?
    A. He finds all the dishes in the dining room smashed.
    B. He notices that someone has left the window open.
    C. He finds a small empty vial lying on the floor.
    D. He notices that one of the china figures is missing.

3. How did Arthur Richmond die?
    A. He was poisoned.
    B. He was hanged.
    C. He was sent on a mission from which he never returned.
    D. He was shot by his lover's husband.

4. Who was Hugo?
    A. He was the uncle of Vera Claythorne's ward, Cyril.
    B. He was a soldier in the war under General Macarthur's command.
    C. Emily Brent was engaged to be married to Hugo.
    D. He built the mansion on Indian Island.

5. What news does Rogers bring to Dr. Armstrong?
    A. One of the china figures in the dining room has disappeared.
    B. His wife won't wake up.
    C. A strong storm is coming and the boat can't make it to the island.
    D. His wife is hysterical and needs a sedative.

6. What are the guests anxious about their first morning on the island?
    A. They suspect each other of murder.
    B. Strange noises kept them all awake during the night.
    C. The boat has not arrived like it usually does.
    D. There is no food cooked for breakfast.

7. What news does Armstrong break to the group immediately following breakfast?
   A. Mrs. Rogers is dead.
   B. The pantry is almost out of food.
   C. The boat will not be coming at all.
   D. A china figure from the dining room table is missing.

8. What conclusion does General Macarthur make about their being lured to the island?
   A. One of the guests on the island must be the mysterious Mr. Owen.
   B. Fred Narracott intends to kill them all one by one.
   C. He is resigned to the fact that none of them will ever leave the island.
   D. The island will soon be totally destroyed by the oncoming storm and they will die.

9. What has Rogers particularly upset at the end of Chapter 6?
   A. A major storm is coming and they are not prepared to withstand it.
   B. A second china figure is missing from the dining room.
   C. The boat will not be coming to bring supplies.
   D. His wife has died.

**Assignment 4**
**Chapters 7-8**

1. What does Emily Brent suspect about Mr. and Mrs. Rogers?
   A. She suspects that they will attempt to leave the island, abandoning the group.
   B. She suspects that they are slowly poisoning the guests with the meals.
   C. She suspects that they killed their employer for the legacy.
   D. She suspects that they are in league with Mr. Owen to destroy them.

2. Who was Beatrice Taylor?
   A. She was General Armstrong's wife.
   B. She was a patient who died on the Dr. Armstrong's operating table.
   C. She was Emily Brent's servant girl who committed suicide after getting pregnant.
   D. She was Vera Claythorne's sister who drowned many years before.

3. How does Armstrong suspect that the Rogers killed their employer?
   A. They withheld necessary medicine, and she died as a result.
   B. They poisoned her tea.
   C. They hired someone to shoot her and make it look like robbery.
   D. They suffocated her in her sleep with a pillow.

4. Why doesn't Lombard believe that Mrs. Rogers killed herself?
   A. She did not have the courage to go through with something like that.
   B. She was already nearly unconscious when she was put under a sedative.
   C. She could not have injected herself with the syringe because she was hysterical.
   D. It is too soon after the death of Tony Marston to be a second suicide.

5. What do Lombard and Armstrong conclude about the nursery rhyme?
   A. It meant nothing; it is merely coincidence.
   B. There must be a murderer hiding on the island.
   C. It is a childish attempt to unnerve the guests.
   D. It is the theme to some crazy murder mystery party and no one is actually dead.

6. After their search, what do Blore, Armstrong, and Lombard discover about the island?
   A. It is shaped like the head of an Indian.
   B. The killer has nowhere to hide expect for the house.
   C. There is a small cave located on the south of the island; there is small boat there.
   D. The north side has steep cliffs, but a set of stairs has been carved into the rocks.

7. Which of the characters has accepted his/her fate and waits patiently for the final outcome?
   A. Emily Brent
   B. Philip Lombard
   C. General Macarthur
   D. Dr. Armstrong

8. How has Emily Brent decided to pass the time?
   A. Reading her Bible
   B. Cooking
   C. Knitting on the terrace
   D. Walking on the shoreline, looking for a boat

9. What is the sound that Blore, Armstrong, and Lombard hear from upstairs?
   A. Judge Wargrave is checking on Emily Brent who had been in her room all day.
   B. Rogers is packing his things in order to move to one of the unoccupied guest rooms.
   C. Emily Brent is sobbing uncontrollably in her room.
   D. Vera is barricading herself in her room by dragging a dresser in front of her door.

10. After searching the entire house, what do Armstrong, Blore, and Lombard conclude?
    A. The murderer must have left using the steps carved into the cliff.
    B. The murderer must be hiding in the cave on the south side of the island.
    C. There is no murderer; the two deaths must have been suicides after all.
    D. There is no one on the island but the occupants of the house.

**Assignment 5**
**Chapters 9-10**

1. What suggestion does Blore make about Mrs. Rogers's death?
    A. Her husband must have killed her to keep her quiet.
    B. She died of natural causes in her sleep.
    C. She had a heart attack because she felt guilty for having killed her employer.
    D. The doctor must have mistakenly given her an overdose of the sedative.

2. What is it that Blore demands to know from Lombard?
    A. How is Lombard related to Mr. Owen?
    B. Why did Lombard poison Tony Marston?
    C. Why did Lombard feel it was necessary to bring a revolver to a social function?
    D. Why didn't Lombard seem as agitated as the rest of the guests?

3. What does Lombard confess actually brought him to Indian Island?
    A. He was paid one hundred guineas to come and keep his eyes open.
    B. He came to assassinate them all.
    C. He knew that Vera Claythorne would be on the island, and he is in love with her.
    D. He is Mr. Owen's son.

4. What observation does Vera make about the weather?
    A. The sea is much calmer now; a boat should be arriving soon.
    B. There is a full moon rising.
    C. The temperature has dropped to freezing, mirroring how cold each person feels.
    D. There is a terrible storm brewing.

5. How does Macarthur die?
    A. He drowns.
    B. He is poisoned.
    C. He is shot.
    D. He is bludgeoned to death.

6. What did Vera and Rogers discover in the dining room right after General Macarthur is found on the beach?
    A. Another china figure is missing from the table.
    B. The lunch food has been left untouched; no one feels like eating.
    C. A bloody hammer is lying under the dining room table.
    D. The window that he had bolted shut is now wide open.

7. What conclusion does Judge Wargrave come to concerning Mr. Owen?
    A. Mr. Owen must be one of the guests.
    B. Mr. Owen is not planning on coming to the island after all; they've been abandoned.
    C. He must be a lunatic and is hunting them one by one; he must be hiding in the attic.
    D. Mr. Owen is pulling one huge publicity stunt to create speculation about the island.

8. Whose name does Emily Brent write in her diary as the murderer?
    A. Beatrice Taylor
    B. Philip Lombard
    C. Vera Claythorne
    D. Dr. Armstrong

9. What item does Rogers claim is missing that has him nervous and upset?
    A. He cannot find the meat cleaver in the kitchen.
    B. A scarlet curtain from the bathroom is missing.
    C. The bottle of cyanide used to kill wasps has disappeared.
    D. The china figures from the dining room keep disappearing.

10. What does Rogers do to prevent the disappearance of any more Indian figurines?
    A. He locks the dining room and pockets the key.
    B. He covers the figurines with a tablecloth so they cannot be easily grabbed.
    C. He breaks all of the remaining figurines.
    D. He takes the figures away and locks them in the pantry.

**Assignment 6**
**Chapters 11-12**

1. What news does Lombard share with Blore when he awakens him in the morning?
   A. Rogers has disappeared.
   B. Mrs. Rogers's body is missing.
   C. He cannot find Emily Brent.
   D. A boat is waiting at the dock to take them back to the mainland.

2. What happens to Rogers?
   A. He is killed with an axe while out chopping wood for the fire.
   B. He oversleeps and does not get up in time to make breakfast.
   C. He has a nervous breakdown.
   D. He gets dizzy and disoriented while walking around the island.

3. Why does Vera begin to laugh uncontrollably?
   A. She is the murderer and now has everyone right where she wants them.
   B. She is hysterical about the death of Tony Marston.
   C. She believes that this is all one big joke and that no one is really dead at all.
   D. She realizes the killer is following the nursery rhyme.

4. What does Blore confess to Lombard?
   A. He killed General Macarthur.
   B. He was hired to make sure no one leaves the island.
   C. He perjured himself and put an innocent man in prison where the man later died.
   D. He is Mr. Owen.

5. Emily Brent dreams of Beatrice Taylor. What is Beatrice doing in the dream?
   A. Beatrice is killing Hugo.
   B. Beatrice is laughing at Emily.
   C. Beatrice is pressing her face against the window and moaning, asking to be let in.
   D. Beatrice is throwing her baby into the sea.

6. While clearing breakfast dishes Emily Brent feels a little giddy, she sits to wait for the feeling to pass. What does she see on the windowpane?
   A. She sees a butterfly crawling up the windowpane.
   B. She sees a bee crawling up the windowpane.
   C. She sees a note left by the killer.
   D. She sees Vera's image.

7. How is Emily Brent murdered?
    A. Emily is injected in the neck with poison.
    B. She is found suffocated in her bedroom.
    C. Emily is thrown from the cliff on the island.
    D. She is found strangled with yarn.

8. Who immediately falls under suspicion for Emily's murder?
    A. Judge Wargrave
    B. Vera
    C. Dr. Armstrong
    D. Mr. Blore

9. What does Mr. Lombard find missing from his bed-table?
    A. His revolver is missing.
    B. The syringe is missing.
    C. His identification papers are missing.
    D. The two figurines he had hidden.

10. Where are the potentially lethal drugs put for safekeeping?
    A. In a chest locked up in the pantry
    B. Locked in a safe in the drawing room wall
    C. Poured down the drain
    D. Locked in a sideboard of the dining room

**Assignment 7**
**Chapters 13-14**

1. Who are the five remaining guests on Indian Island?
    A. Rogers, Blore, Lombard, Claythorne, Armstrong
    B. Wargrave, Macarthur, Lombard, Claythorne, Armstrong
    C. Wargrave, Blore, Lombard, Claythorne, Armstrong
    D. Wargrave, Blore, Lombard, Brent, Armstrong

2. Which of the characters is said to look like "a wary old tortoise"?
    A. Mr. Blore
    B. Vera Claythorne
    C. Philip Lombard
    D. Judge Wargrave

3. Vera goes to her room to bathe her aching head and temples in cold water. What causes her screams of terror?
    A. She discovers a bloody, dead body in her room.
    B. She is attacked in the dark.
    C. She sees the ghost of Mrs. Rogers.
    D. She walks into seaweed hanging in her room. She thinks it is a wet, clammy hand.

4. When Mr. Justice Wargrave is discovered dead what is strange about his appearance?
    A. He is holding the missing revolver.
    B. He is dressed as a judge with a grey wig (the missing yarn) and a scarlet "robe" (the missing oilsilk).
    C. He is dressed like a General.
    D. He appears to be sleeping.

5. What foods are the survivors reduced to eating?
    A. Canned sardines
    B. Macaroni and cheese
    C. Tinned tongue
    D. Salted pork

6. Who finds the revolver?
    A. Vera Claythorne
    B. Philip Lombard
    C. Mr. Blore
    D. Judge Wargrave

7. What does Vera see in her room that she had not noticed before?
   A. A picture of Mr. Owen above the bed
   B. A copy of the nursery rhyme
   C. A secret panel leading to the dining room
   D. A large hook in the ceiling

8. Who hears someone sneaking around the house and decides to investigate?
   A. Dr. Armstrong
   B. Vera Claythorne
   C. Mr. Blore
   D. Philip Lombard

9. Who disappears at the end of Chapter 14?
   A. Philip Lombard
   B. Vera Claythorne
   C. Mr. Blore
   D. Dr. Armstrong

**Assignment 8**
**Chapters 15-16**

1. What change has occurred in the weather at the opening of Chapter 15?
   A. A hurricane is brewing.
   B. It has begun to snow; it mirrors the cold emotions on the island.
   C. The thunder and lightning has become more fierce.
   D. The sun is shining and the storm is over.

2. How does Lombard suggest the survivors make contact with people on the mainland?
   A. He suggests using the telephone, but it is disconnected.
   B. He suggests using a mirror to heliograph an S O S.
   C. He suggests standing on the beach waving white clothing as flags.
   D. He thinks they could build a signal fire when the rain stops.

3. What does Vera suddenly remember about the nursery rhyme that makes the party think that Dr. Armstrong is still alive?
   A. Armstrong never went to Chancery.
   B. She remembers the line about the red herring and believes they have been tricked.
   C. A person is too large to be swallowed by a tiny fish, so Armstrong cannot be dead.
   D. Remembering how the fourth Indian boy died, it doesn't fit Armstrong's disappearance.

4. What happens to Blore?
   A. His skull is crushed by a marble clock that is in the shape of a bear.
   B. He is shot by Philip Lombard.
   C. He drowns trying to swim away from the island.
   D. He escapes the island in a small boat found earlier in a cave.

5. What do Vera and Lombard find that ends up pitting them against each other?
   A. They find the larder is nearly out of food; there isn't enough for two people.
   B. They find a boat that is only big enough for one person.
   C. They find Armstrong's drowned body by the beach.
   D. They find the revolver lying on the beach.

6. When staring at him on the beach, to what does Vera compare Lombard's face?
   A. An angel
   B. A hawk
   C. A mask
   D. A wolf

7. What does Vera do when she and Lombard are dragging Dr. Armstrong's body away from the sea?
    A. She faints from exhaustion.
    B. She takes the revolver from Lombard's pocket.
    C. She pushes Lombard into the sea.
    D. She attempts to kiss Lombard, but he pushes her away.

8. What happens to Philip Lombard?
    A. Vera pushes him into the sea.
    B. He escapes in the tiny boat he and Vera had found.
    C. He falls in love with Vera.
    D. Vera shoots him.

9. Vera believes someone is waiting for her in her bedroom. Who?
    A. Cyril
    B. Isaac Morris
    C. Philip
    D. Hugo

10. How does Vera Claythorne die?
    A. She hangs herself.
    B. Philip Lombard shoots her.
    C. She falls and breaks her neck.
    D. She takes poison.

**Assignment 9**
**Epilogue and Letter**

1. What does the Assistant Commissioner of Scotland Yard find on Indian Island?
    A. The island is completely deserted.
    B. There are ten dead bodies and not a living soul on the island.
    C. The mansion has been burned down.
    D. He finds Philip Lombard barely alive, but breathing.

2. Identify Isaac Morris.
    A. He is the chief of police in Sticklehaven.
    B. He is Vera's fiance.
    C. He made the arrangements for the purchase of the island for an unnamed third party.
    D. He is the true owner of Indian Island.

3. Why had the people of Sticklehaven not attempted to make contact with anyone on Indian Island?
    A. They hadn't noticed anything peculiar going on, so they didn't even think about the island.
    B. The storm had made all communication impossible, even though they tried.
    C. They didn't know the owner, so they didn't bother.
    D. Mr. Morris told them that there was a contest on the island and to ignore all signals.

4. Why did Fred Narracott ignore the edict and take his boat over there?
    A. He had been paid to return on a specific date.
    B. As the one who brought supplies, he knew that they were going to run out of food soon.
    C. He thought the guests looked too normal, and the S O S made him suspicious.
    D. He had received a strange telephone call from the island asking him to hurry over.

5. What makes the inspector absolutely certain that Vera Claythorne had not committed the murders?
    A. She was not strong enough to have killed the men on the island.
    B. She was one of the earliest ones to die.
    C. They found a signed confession from the murderer on the dining room table.
    D. Although she had hanged herself, the chair she had used was back by the wall.

6. How do the police manage to solve the crime of Indian Island?
   A. They find the confession on the dining room table next to the ten Indian boy figurines.
   B. They hire Sherlock Holmes to solve the mystery.
   C. A fisherman finds a confession in a sealed bottle floating in the water.
   D. Philip Lombard is still alive and he confessed.

7. Who was the murderer on Indian Island?
   A. Philip Lombard
   B. Vera Claythorne
   C. Judge Wargrave
   D. Emily Brent

8. Why did the murderer decide on these particular ten victims?
   A. He picked them at random from the telephone book.
   B. They had all come before him in trial yet were not convicted.
   C. All were guilty of murder, yet the law could not touch them.
   D. At one time or another, all had vacationed at a certain hotel.

9. Which of the killer's victims did not actually die on Indian Island?
   A. Dr. Armstrong
   B. Isaac Morris
   C. Emily Brent
   D. Mrs. Rogers

10. How did the killer manage to complete the scheme without being caught by the others?
    A. She seduced Philip Lombard into helping her.
    B. He hid in the cave on the south side of the island.
    C. He managed to hide in a closet behind a fake wall in the dining room.
    D. Wargrave faked his death with the help of Dr. Armstrong.

# ANSWER KEY: STUDY QUESTIONS *And Then There Were None*

|    | 1 | 2 | 3 | 4 | 5 | 6 | 7 | 8 | 9 |
|----|---|---|---|---|---|---|---|---|---|
| 1  | D | C | D | C | D | A | C | D | B |
| 2  | A | A | D | C | C | A | D | B | C |
| 3  | C | B | C | A | A | D | D | B | D |
| 4  | A | D | A | D | D | C | B | A | C |
| 5  | C | D | B | B | D | C | C | C | D |
| 6  | D | A | C | B | A | B | B | D | C |
| 7  | D | D | A | C | A | A | D | B | C |
| 8  | B | C | C | C | A | C | C | D | C |
| 9  |   | B | B | B | B | A | D | D | B |
| 10 |   | C |   | D | A | A |   | A | D |
| 11 |   | B |   |   |   |   |   |   |   |

# VOCABULARY WORKSHEETS

# VOCABULARY ASSIGNMENT 1 *And Then There Were None*

Part I: Using Prior Knowledge and Contextual Clues

Below are the sentences in which the vocabulary words appear in the text. Read the sentence. Use any clues you can find in the sentence combined with your prior knowledge, and write what you think the underlined words mean on the lines provided.

1. The unfortunate fact that the new third wife of the American millionaire was a bad sailor had led to the <u>subsequent</u> putting up of the house and island for sale.

2. "After all, people don't like a Coroner's <u>Inquest</u>, even if the Coroner did acquit me of all blame!"

3. Her father, a Colonel of the old school, had been particular about <u>deportment</u>.

4. There had been a time when he sat in his consulting room in Harley Street--and waited--waited through the empty days for his <u>venture</u> to succeed or fail....

5. "There's a squall ahead. I can smell it."
   "Maybe you're right," said Mr. Blore <u>pacifically</u>.

6. Four voices gave assent--and then immediately afterwards gave quick <u>surreptitious</u> glances at each other.

7. Their guide led them to a small stone <u>jetty</u>. Alongside it a motor boat was lying.

8. A car so fantastically powerful, so <u>superlatively</u> beautiful that it had all the nature of an apparition.

9. "All doctors are damned fools. Harley Street ones are the worst of the lot." And his mind dwelt <u>malevolently</u> on a recent interview he had had with a suave personage in that very street.

10. Rising, she pinned a <u>cairngorm</u> brooch at her neck, and went down to dinner.

*And Then There Were None* Vocabulary Worksheet Assignment 1 Continued

Part II: Determining the Meaning -- Match the vocabulary words to their dictionary definitions.

____ 1. SUBSEQUENT    A. An investigation made by a coroner into the cause of a death

____ 2. INQUEST    B. Demeanor; conduct; behavior

____ 3. DEPORTMENT    C. Undertaking involving uncertainty as to the outcome

____ 4. VENTURE    D. In an evil, harmful, or injurious manner

____ 5. PACIFICALLY    E. Smoky-yellow to dark brown or black variety of quartz, used as a gem stone

____ 6. SURREPTITIOUS    F. Of the highest kind, quality, or order; surpassing all else or others

____ 7. JETTY    G. Peaceably, mildly, calmly, or quietly

____ 8. SUPERLATIVELY    H. Wharf; landing pier

____ 9. MALEVOLENTLY    I. Taking pains to avoid being observed; cautious; stealthy

____ 10. CAIRNGORM    J. Occurring or coming later or after

VOCABULARY ASSIGNMENT 2 *And Then There Were None*

Part I: Using Prior Knowledge and Contextual Clues

Below are the sentences in which the vocabulary words appear in the text. Read the sentence. Use any clues you can find in the sentence combined with your prior knowledge, and write what you think the underlined words mean on the lines provided.

1. Blore studied with naive surprise a statuette in brass--wondering perhaps if its bizarre angularities were really supposed to be the female figure.

   _____

2. You are charged with the following indictments:

   _____

3. The mouth of the trumpet was against the wall, and Lombard, pushing it aside, indicated where two or three small holes had been unobtrusively bored through the wall.

   _____

4. Mr. Justice Wargrave took charge of the proceedings. The room became an impromptu court of law.

   _____

5. "No, a colleague of mine was mentioned in the letter."
   The judge said, "To give verisimilitude . . . Yes, and that colleague, I presume, was momentarily out of touch with you?"

   _____

6. "In passing sentence of death I concurred with the verdict."

   _____

7. "Richmond was one of my officers. I sent him on a reconnaissance. He was killed."

   _____

8. The manservant, Rogers, had been moistening his lips and twisting his hands. He said now in a low deferential voice: "If I might just say a word, sir."

   _____

9. "Miss Brady left us a legacy in recognition of our faithful services."

   _____

10. There was silence in the room. Everyone was looking, covertly or openly, at Emily Brent.

    _____

*And Then There Were None* Vocabulary Worksheet Assignment 2 Continued

Part II: Determining the Meaning -- Match the vocabulary words to their dictionary definitions.

____ 1. ANGULARITIES     A. The appearance or semblance of truth; likelihood; probability

____ 2. INDICTMENTS     B. Search made for useful military information in the field

____ 3. UNOBTRUSIVELY     C. Written statements charging a party with the commission of a crime

____ 4. IMPROMPTU     D. Showing regard or respect

____ 5. VERISIMILITUDE     E. Gift of property or money through a will; a bequest

____ 6. CONCURRED     F. Sharp corners; angular outlines

____ 7. RECONNAISSANCE     G. Was of the same opinion; agreed

____ 8. DEFERENTIAL     H. Made or done without previous preparation

____ 9. LEGACY     I. Secretly; in a concealed manner

____ 10. COVERTLY     J. In a manner that is not undesirably noticeable or blatant

VOCABULARY ASSIGNMENT 3 *And Then There Were None*

Part I: Using Prior Knowledge and Contextual Clues
Below are the sentences in which the vocabulary words appear in the text. Read the sentence. Use any clues you can find in the sentence combined with your prior knowledge, and write what you think the underlined words mean on the lines provided.

1. "You can call it choking of you like. He died of <u>asphyxiation</u> right enough."

   _____

2. Together Armstrong and Lombard had carried the <u>inert</u> body of Anthony Marston to his bedroom and had laid him there covered over with a sheet.

   _____

3. Any one could see with half an eye that the woman was as <u>pious</u> as could be--the kind that was hand and glove with parsons.

   _____

4. Cyril wasn't really strong. A puny child--no <u>stamina</u>. The kind of child, perhaps, who wouldn't live to grow up. . . .

   _____

5. As she passed the mantelpiece, she looked up at the framed <u>doggerel</u>.

   _____

6. Ah! That was better. A young <u>probationer</u> was pulling off the handkerchief.

   _____

7. General Macarthur and the judge had been pacing the terrace outside, exchanging <u>desultory</u> comments on the political situation.

   _____

8. As they went down the steep slope Blore said to Lombard in a <u>ruminating</u> voice: "You know, it beats me--why that young fellow wanted to do himself in! I've been worrying about it all night."

   _____

9. "Mrs. Rogers died in her sleep." There were startled and shocked <u>ejaculations</u>.

   _____

10. Along the terrace, then down the slope toward the sea--<u>obliquely</u>--to the end of the island where loose rocks went out into the water.

    _____

*And Then There Were None* Vocabulary Worksheet Assignment 3 Continued

Part II: Determining the Meaning -- Match the vocabulary words to their dictionary definitions.

____ 1. ASPHYXIATION  A. Sudden, short exclamations, especially brief, pious utterances or prayers

____ 2. INERT  B. Having a slanting or sloping direction, course, or position; in an inclined way

____ 3. PIOUS  C. Unable to move or act

____ 4. STAMINA  D. Crudely or irregularly fashioned verse, often of a humorous or burlesque nature

____ 5. DOGGEREL  E. Reflecting on over and over again; turning a matter over in the mind

____ 6. PROBATIONER  F. Death by choking, smothering, or suffocating

____ 7. DESULTORY  G. Physical or moral strength to resist or withstand illness, fatigue, or hardship; endurance

____ 8. RUMINATING  H. Lacking in consistency or visible order; disconnected

____ 9. EJACULATIONS  I. Nurse in training who is undergoing a trial period

____ 10. OBLIQUELY  J. Characterized by a hypocritical concern with virtue or religious devotion

VOCABULARY ASSIGNMENT 4 *And Then There Were None*

Part I: Using Prior Knowledge and Contextual Clues

Below are the sentences in which the vocabulary words appear in the text. Read the sentence. Use any clues you can find in the sentence combined with your prior knowledge, and write what you think the underlined words mean on the lines provided.

1. Vera listened with interest. Miss Brent continued serenely: "Beatrice Taylor was in service with me."

2. "I? I had nothing with which to reproach myself."

3. "Do you accept Blore's theory?"
   Philip puffed smoke into the air. He said: "It's perfectly feasible--taken alone."

4. "When an attack comes on, an ampoule of amyl nitrite is broken and it is inhaled."

5. "Wargrave murdered Edward Seton all right, murdered him as surely as if he'd stuck a stiletto through him!"

6. He paid no attention to the approach of the searchers. His oblivion of them made one at least faintly uncomfortable.

7. "Nobody could have clambered down here, I suppose?"
   Armstrong shook his head.
   "I doubt it. It's pretty sheer."

8. Vera had been restless all the morning. She had avoided Emily Brent with a kind of shuddering aversion.

9. "Wonderful animal, the good servant. Carries on with an impassive countenance."

10. They all heard it. Armstrong grasped Blore's arm. Lombard held up an admonitory finger.

*And Then There Were None* Vocabulary Worksheet Assignment 4 Continued

Part II: Determining the Meaning -- Match the vocabulary words to their dictionary definitions.

____ 1. SERENELY	A. Climbed with difficulty, especially on all fours

____ 2. REPROACH	B. Look or expression of the face

____ 3. FEASIBLE	C. Find fault with; blame; censure

____ 4. AMPOULE	D. Sealed glass or plastic bulb containing solutions for hypodermic injection

____ 5. STILETTO	E. A small dagger with a slender, tapering blade

____ 6. OBLIVION	F. Serving to warn, especially to correct

____ 7. CLAMBERED	G. In a calm, peaceful, or tranquil manner

____ 8. AVERSION	H. Capable of being done, effected, or accomplished

____ 9. COUNTENANCE	I. Strong feeling of dislike, opposition, or repugnance

____ 10. ADMONITORY	J. State of being completely forgotten or unknown

VOCABULARY ASSIGNMENT 5 *And Then There Were None*

Part I: Using Prior Knowledge and Contextual Clues

Below are the sentences in which the vocabulary words appear in the text. Read the sentence. Use any clues you can find in the sentence combined with your prior knowledge, and write what you think the underlined words mean on the lines provided.

1. "There is plenty of food, sir--of a tinned variety. The <u>larder</u> is very well stocked."

   _____

2. He darted quick looks from under his bushy eyebrows at the other occupants of the dining-room. He said, "You've had an active morning." There was a faint <u>malicious</u> pleasure in his voice.

   _____

3. It was as they had left it. There was a sweet course ready on the <u>sideboard</u> untasted.

   _____

4. "To put it simply, is there among us one or more persons who could not possibly have administered either Cyanide to Anthony Marston, or an overdose of sleeping <u>draught</u> to Mrs. Rogers, . . . ."

   _____

5. "No good can come from <u>recrimination</u>. Facts are what we have to deal with."

   _____

6. "He wouldn't have had time during that brief <u>interval</u> when I left him--not, that is, unless he fairly hared down there and back again, and I doubt if he's in good enough training to do that and show no signs of it."

   _____

7. It flashed across Dr. Armstrong's mind that an old man like the judge, was far more <u>tenacious</u> of life than a younger man would be.

   _____

8. "And I have lost two <u>skeins</u> of my grey knitting-wool."

   _____

9. "What kind of a curtain was it?"
   "Scarlet <u>oilsilk</u>, sir. It went with the scarlet tiles."

   _____

10. Inside the room, the <u>pall</u> of fear had fallen anew.

    _____

*And Then There Were None* Vocabulary Worksheet Assignment 5 Continued

Part II: Determining the Meaning -- Match the vocabulary words to their dictionary definitions.

____ 1.  LARDER          A. Dose of liquid medicine

____ 2.  MALICIOUS       B. Act of accusing in return

____ 3.  SIDEBOARD       C. Piece of dining room furniture having drawers and shelves for linens and tableware

____ 4.  DRAUGHT         D. Deliberately harmful or spiteful

____ 5.  RECRIMINATION   E. Lengths of thread or yarn wound in loose, long coils

____ 6.  INTERVAL        F. Heavy, water-resistant fabric

____ 7.  TENACIOUS       G. Room or place where food is stored; pantry

____ 8.  SKEINS          H. Holding fast; characterized by keeping a firm hold

____ 9.  OILSILK         I. In between period of time

____ 10. PALL            J. Anything that covers, shrouds, or overspreads, esp. with darkness or gloom

VOCABULARY ASSIGNMENT 6 *And Then There Were None*

Part I: Using Prior Knowledge and Contextual Clues

Below are the sentences in which the vocabulary words appear in the text. Read the sentence. Use any clues you can find in the sentence combined with your prior knowledge, and write what you think the underlined words mean on the lines provided.

1. Phil Lombard said affably, "Sleeping round the clock? Well, shows you've got an easy conscience."

   _____

2. Rogers' room, as Philip Lombard had already ascertained, was untenanted.

   _____

3. Miss Brent was raking out the stove. Vera was cutting the rind off the bacon.

   _____

4. "And then she was out--in her mackintosh, said she's been down to look at the sea."

   _____

5. It was as though a sharp little gimlet had run into the solid congealed mass of Emily Brent's brain.

   _____

6. "I don't wish to take anything--anything at all. I will just sit here quietly till the giddiness passes off."

   _____

7. "I think we should summon Miss Brent to join our conclave."

   _____

8. And then they saw her face--suffused with blood, with blue lips and staring eyes.

   _____

9. "One of us is a murderer. The position is fraught with grave danger."

   _____

10. Philip strode across to the bed-side table and jerked open the drawer. Then he recoiled with an oath. The drawer of the bed table was empty.

    _____

*And Then There Were None* Vocabulary Worksheet Assignment 6 Continued

Part II: Determining the Meaning -- Match the vocabulary words to their dictionary definitions.

____ 1.  AFFABLY          A. Dizziness

____ 2.  UNTENANTED       B. Thick and firm outer coat or covering

____ 3.  RIND             C. In a friendly, cordial manner

____ 4.  MACKINTOSH       D. Raincoat

____ 5.  GIMLET           E. Unoccupied; not leased to or occupied by a tenant

____ 6.  GIDDINESS        F. Filled or laden (with)

____ 7.  CONCLAVE         G. Spread through or over, as with liquid, color, or light

____ 8.  SUFFUSED         H. Private or secret meeting

____ 9.  FRAUGHT          I. Small tool for boring holes

____ 10. RECOILED         J. Shrunk back, as in fear or repugnance

VOCABULARY ASSIGNMENT 7 *And Then There Were None*

Part I: Using Prior Knowledge and Contextual Clues
Below are the sentences in which the vocabulary words appear in the text. Read the sentence. Use any clues you can find in the sentence combined with your prior knowledge, and write what you think the underlined words mean on the lines provided.

1. There was little <u>pretence</u> now--no formal veneer of conversation. They were five enemies linked together by a mutual instinct of self-preservation.

   _____

2. The other three had whiskey--opening a fresh bottle and using a <u>siphon</u> from a nailed up case.

   _____

3. <u>Aeons</u> of time seemed to pass. They were offering her something to drink--pressing the glass against her lips.

   _____

4. His expression did not alter. He said <u>dubiously</u>, "H'm, tastes all right."

   _____

5. "Five little Indian boys going in for law; one got in <u>Chancery</u> and then there were four."

   _____

6. There were sounds of bolts and locks, of the moving of furniture. Four frightened people were <u>barricaded</u> in until morning.

   _____

7. He was like a wild boar waiting to charge. He felt no <u>inclination</u> to sleep.

   _____

8. For all his <u>sagacity</u>, for all his caution and astuteness, the old judge had gone the way of the rest.

   _____

9. He . . . detached the plug of the electric lamp by his bed, and picked it up winding the flex round it. It was a chromium affair with a heavy <u>ebonite</u> base--a useful weapon.

   _____

10. More, he might actually set the house on fire. . . . Yes, that would be a possibility. Lure the other two men out of the house, then, having previously laid a trail of <u>petrol</u>, he might set light to it.

    _____

*And Then There Were None* Vocabulary Worksheet Assignment 7 Continued

Part II: Determining the Meaning -- Match the vocabulary words to their dictionary definitions.

____ 1. PRETENCE      A. False show of something

____ 2. SIPHON        B. Acuteness of mental discernment and soundness of judgment

____ 3. AEONS         C. Gasoline

____ 4. DUBIOUSLY     D. Indefinitely long period of time

____ 5. CHANCERY      E. In a doubtful manner

____ 6. BARRICADED    F. Division of the High Court of Justice of Great Britain

____ 7. INCLINATION   G. Hard, non-resilient rubber formed by vulcanizing natural rubber

____ 8. SAGACITY      H. Disposition or bent, esp. of the mind or will; a liking or preference

____ 9. EBONITE       I. Pipe or tube to draw off or convey liquid through

____ 10. PETROL       J. Blocked with a defensive barrier

VOCABULARY ASSIGNMENT 8 *And Then There Were None*

Part I: Using Prior Knowledge and Contextual Clues

Below are the sentences in which the vocabulary words appear in the text. Read the sentence. Use any clues you can find in the sentence combined with your prior knowledge, and write what you think the underlined words mean on the lines provided.

1. "We'll try heliographing today with a mirror from the highest point of the island. Some bright lad wandering the cliff will recognize S O S when he sees it, I hope."

   _____

2. "Only three little Indian boys left on the dinner table. It looks as though Armstrong had got his quietus."

   _____

3. "Armstrong's not armed, you know, and anyway Blore is twice a match for him in physique and he's very much on his guard."

   _____

4. A sudden feeling of lassitude, of intense weariness, spread over Vera's limbs.

   _____

5. The terrace was peaceful and innocuous-looking in the sunshine.

   _____

6. "How was it worked--that trick with the marble bear?"
   He shrugged his shoulders. "A conjuring trick, my dear--a very good one. . . ."

   _____

7. "So that's the reason for your womanly solicitude! You wanted to pick my pocket."

   _____

8. By her own quick-wittedness and adroitness, she had turned the tables on her would-be destroyer.

   _____

9. The little china figure fell from her hand. It rolled unheeded and broke against the fender.

   _____

10. Like an automaton Vera moved forward. This was the end--here where the cold wet hand (Cyril's hand, of course) had touched her throat. . . .

    _____

*And Then There Were None* Vocabulary Worksheet Assignment 8 Continued

Part II: Determining the Meaning -- Match the vocabulary words to their dictionary definitions.

____ 1. HELIOGRAPHING     A. Disregarded; ignored

____ 2. QUIETUS     B. Attitude expressing excessive attentiveness

____ 3. PHYSIQUE     C. Expertise or nimbleness in the use of the hands or body

____ 4. LASSITUDE     D. Transmitting messages by reflecting sunlight

____ 5. INNOCUOUS     E. Harmless

____ 6. CONJURING     F. Weariness of body or mind from strain; lack of energy

____ 7. SOLICITUDE     G. Physical or bodily structure, appearance

____ 8. ADROITNESS     H. Discharge or release from life

____ 9. UNHEEDED     I. Mechanical figure; robot

____ 10. AUTOMATON     J. Affecting or influencing as if by invocation or a magic spell

# VOCABULARY ASSIGNMENT 9 *And Then There Were None*

Part I: Using Prior Knowledge and Contextual Clues

Below are the sentences in which the vocabulary words appear in the text. Read the sentence. Use any clues you can find in the sentence combined with your prior knowledge, and write what you think the underlined words mean on the lines provided.

1. "Who provisioned the island and made all the necessary arrangements?"

   _____

2. "It was sent to U.N. Owen, Esq. c/o Isaac Morris, and was understood to be required for the amateur performance of a hitherto unacted play."

   _____

3. ". . . a woman called Clees who was operated on by him way back in 1925 at Leithmore, when he was attached to the hospital there. Peritonitis and she died on the operating table."

   _____

4. "Old Wargrave made some notes--dry legal cryptic stuff, but quite clear."

   _____

5. "We knew Blore--and he was not the man that you'd ever accuse of a desire for abstract justice."

   _____

6. It is abhorrent to me that an innocent person or creature should suffer or die by an act of mine.

   _____

7. On at least two occasions I stopped cases where to my mind the accused was palpably innocent, directing the jury that there was no case.

   _____

8. My imagination, sternly checked by the exigencies of my profession, waxed secretly to colossal force.

   _____

9. It must be a fantastical crime--something stupendous--out of the common!

   _____

10. . . . the rhyme of the ten little Indian boys. It had fascinated me as a child of two--the inexorable diminishment--the sense of inevitability.

    _____

*And Then There Were None* Vocabulary Worksheet Assignment 9 Continued

Part II: Determining the Meaning -- Match the vocabulary words to their dictionary definitions.

____ 1. PROVISIONED    A. Pressing or urgent situations

____ 2. HITHERTO       B. Up to this time; until now

____ 3. PERITONITIS    C. Plainly seen, heard, or perceived; obviously

____ 4. CRYPTIC        D. Causing amazement; astounding; marvelous

____ 5. ABSTRACT       E. Theoretical; not applied or practical

____ 6. ABHORRENT      F. Detestable; loathsome; hateful

____ 7. PALPABLY       G. Unable to be avoided, evaded, or escaped

____ 8. EXIGENCIES     H. Mysterious in meaning; puzzling; ambiguous

____ 9. STUPENDOUS     I. Provided a stock of necessary supplies, especially food

____ 10. INEVITABILITY J. Inflammation of the membrane surrounding the abdominal cavity

## VOCABULARY ANSWER KEY - *And Then There Were None*

|    | 1 | 2 | 3 | 4 | 5 | 6 | 7 | 8 | 9 |
|----|---|---|---|---|---|---|---|---|---|
| 1  | J | F | F | G | G | C | A | D | I |
| 2  | A | C | C | C | D | E | I | H | B |
| 3  | B | J | J | H | C | B | D | G | J |
| 4  | C | H | G | D | A | D | E | F | H |
| 5  | G | A | D | E | B | I | F | E | E |
| 6  | I | G | I | J | I | A | J | J | F |
| 7  | H | B | H | A | H | H | H | B | C |
| 8  | F | D | E | I | E | G | B | C | A |
| 9  | D | E | A | B | F | F | G | A | D |
| 10 | E | I | B | F | J | J | C | I | G |

# DAILY LESSONS

# LESSON ONE

## Objectives

1. To become familiar with the elements of the murder mystery genre
2. To introduced the first murder mystery, "The Murders in the Rue Morgue" by Edgar Allan Poe
3. To introduce Dame Agatha Christie
4. To introduce Christie's novel, *And Then There Were None*
5. To preview the vocabulary worksheet and study guide questions for chapters 1 and 2
6. To read chapters 1 and 2

## Activity 1

Ask students to brainstorm what makes a good mystery; they should list at least three elements that should be included. Students share ideas aloud and write them on the chalk board. For any of the elements they may have missed, ask leading questions so that students can come up with the answers themselves.

## Activity 2

Also, read aloud the story "The Murders in the Rue Morgue" by Edgar Allan Poe (touted as the first murder mystery) which led to the mystery genre as we know it. (This story is easily accessible on the Internet). Ask students to take notes of clues they hear in the story as it is being read. Before coming to the final climax in which the murderer is revealed, ask students who they think might have committed the brutal murders and how. What clues do they have to substantiate their claims? Then finish the tale and discuss the ending. How many students were on the right track? How many were misled by red-herrings or misinterpreted clues? Transition into brief notes about the author of the mystery they are about to read, Dame Agatha Christie (see Introductory Materials for this LitPlan).

## Activity 3

Distribute the materials students will use in this unit. Explain in detail how students are to use these materials.

**Study Guides** Students should read the study guide questions for each reading assignment prior to beginning the reading assignment to get a feeling for what events and ideas are important in the section they are about to read. After reading the section, students will (as a class or individually) answer the questions to review the important events and ideas from that section of the book. Students should keep the study guides as study materials for the unit test. **Preview the study questions for Chapters 1 and 2 while students have their study guides out.**

**Vocabulary** Prior to each reading assignment, students will do vocabulary work related to the section of the book they are about to read. Following the completion of the reading of the book, there will be a vocabulary review of all the words used in the vocabulary assignments. Students should keep their vocabulary work as study materials for the unit test. **Do the worksheet for Chapters 1 and 2 orally with the class to show students how the worksheets should be done.**

**Reading Assignment Sheet** You need to fill in the reading assignment sheet to let students know by when their reading has to be completed. You can either write the assignment sheet up on a side blackboard or bulletin board and leave it there for students to see each day, or you can photocopy schedules for each student to have. In either case, you should advise students to become very familiar with the reading assignments so they know what is expected of them.

**Extra Activities Center** The Unit Resource Materials portion of this LitPlan contains suggestions for an extra library of related books and articles in your classroom as well as crossword and word search puzzles. Make an extra activities center in your room where you will keep these materials for students to use. (Bring the books and articles in from the library and keep several copies of the puzzles on hand.) Explain to students that these materials are available for students to use when they finish reading assignments or other class work early.

**Non-fiction Assignment Sheet** Explain to students that they each are to read at least one non-fiction piece from the in-class library at some time during the unit. Students will fill out a Non-fiction Assignment Sheet after completing the reading to help you (the teacher) evaluate their reading experiences and to help the students think about and evaluate their own reading experiences.

**Books** Each school has its own rules and regulations regarding student use of school books. Advise students of the procedures that are normal for your school. Preview the book. Look at the covers, front-matter, and index.

Activity 4
Students should read chapters 1 and 2 prior to the next class meeting. If time remains in this class, they may begin this assignment.

# LESSON TWO

Objectives
1. To review the main ideas and events from chapters 1 and 2
2. To preview the study guide questions and vocabulary for Chapters 3 and 4
3. To evaluate students' oral reading
4. To read Chapters 3 and 4

Activity 1
Give students a few minutes to formulate answers to the study questions for Chapters 1 and 2 and then discuss the answers to the questions in detail. Write the answers on the board or overhead transparency so students can have the correct answers for study purposes.

**NOTE:** It is a good practice in public speaking and leadership skills for individual students to take charge of leading the discussions of the study questions. Perhaps a different student could go to the front of the class and lead the discussion each day that the study questions are discussed in this unit. Of course, you should guide the discussion when appropriate and try to fill in any gaps students may leave. The study questions could really be handled in a number of different ways, including in small groups with group reports following. Occasionally you may want to use the multiple choice questions as quizzes to check students' reading comprehension. As a short review now and then, students could pair up for the first (or last, if you have time left at the end of a class period) few minutes of class to quiz each other from the study questions. Mix up the methods of reviewing the materials and checking comprehension throughout the unit so students don't get bored just answering the questions the same way each day. Variety in methods will also help address the different learning styles of your students.

From now on in this unit, the directions will simply say, "Discuss the answers to the study questions in detail as previously directed." You will choose the method of preparation and discussion each day based on what best suits you and your class.

Activity 2
Do the vocabulary worksheet for Chapters 3 and 4 orally together in class.

Activity 3
Have students read Chapters 3 and 4 of *And Then There Were None* out loud in class. You probably know the best way to get readers with your class; pick students at random, ask for volunteers, or use whatever method works best for your group. If you have not yet completed an oral reading evaluation for your students this period, this would be a good opportunity to do so. A form is included with this unit for your convenience.

If you do not finish reading Chapters 3 and 4 during class, students should finish the assignment prior to the next class meeting.

ORAL READING EVALUATION - *And Then There Were None*

Name _____ Class _____ Date _____

| SKILL | EXCELLENT | GOOD | AVERAGE | FAIR | POOR |
|---|---|---|---|---|---|
| Fluency | 5 | 4 | 3 | 2 | 1 |
| Clarity | 5 | 4 | 3 | 2 | 1 |
| Audibility | 5 | 4 | 3 | 2 | 1 |
| Pronunciation | 5 | 4 | 3 | 2 | 1 |
|  | 5 | 4 | 3 | 2 | 1 |
|  | 5 | 4 | 3 | 2 | 1 |

Total     Grade

Comments:

# LESSON THREE

### Objectives
1. To review the main ideas and events of Chapters 3 and 4
2. To improve research skills through use of the library/media center
3. To lay groundwork for Writing Assignment 1
4. To preview the study questions and do the vocabulary work for Chapters 5 and 6

### Activity 1
Discuss the answers to the study questions for Chapters 3 and 4 as previously directed.

### Activity 2
Take students to the school's library/media center. Distribute the Non-fiction Assignment Sheet and discuss the directions in detail. Give students ample time to complete the assignment.

### Activity 3
Tell students that prior to the next class period they should preview the study questions for Chapters 5 and 6, do the pre-reading vocabulary worksheet for Chapters 5 and 6, and read those same chapters. Students who complete their non-fiction assignment early should begin on the work for Chapters 5 and 6.

# NON-FICTION READING ASSIGNMENT
*And Then There Were None*

While in the Library/Media Center, students are to research unsolved murder cases. They are to read articles surrounding a case of their choice and speculate (based on the information they have gathered) on who may have committed the crime and why.

They should be sure to include the following in their research:

- The name of the murdered person
- The method of demise (describe the crime in detail)
- The list of possible suspects
- Possible motives for each suspect
- Evidence/clues produced by the police
- The reason that the case is still marked "unsolved"
- The student's idea of the guilty party

This information will later be the basis for their first writing assignment.

# NON-FICTION ASSIGNMENT SHEET
(To be completed after reading the required non-fiction article)

Name _____ Date _____

Title of Non-fiction Read _____

Written By                        Publication Date

I. Factual Summary: Write a short summary of the piece you read.

II. Vocabulary
    1. With which vocabulary words in the piece did you encounter some degree of difficulty?

    2. How did you resolve your lack of understanding with these words?

III. Interpretation: What was the main point the author wanted you to get from reading his work?

IV. Criticism
    1. With which points of the piece did you agree or find easy to accept? Why?

    2. With which points of the piece did you disagree or find difficult to believe? Why?

V. Personal Response: Who do you believe committed the crime? Why? What evidence can you produce to support your claim?

# LESSON FOUR

<u>Objectives</u>
1. To review the main events and ideas from Chapters 5 and 6
2. To improve public speaking skills
3. To share information about the researched unsolved mysteries
4. To study the form of a mystery short story through writing one
5. To preview the study questions and do the pre-reading vocabulary work for Chapters 7 and 8
6. To read Chapters 7 and 8

<u>Activity 1</u>
Discuss the answers to the study questions for Chapters 5 and 6 as previously directed.

<u>Activity 2</u>
Ask each student to give a brief oral report about the non-fiction articles he/she read for this assignment. Your criteria for evaluating this report will vary depending on the level of your students.

Start with one student's report. Once the student has completed the report, he/she may ask the class for three ideas about how to "solve" the unsolved mystery. (Students may use these ideas as springboards when completing Writing Assignment #1.)

<u>Activity 3</u>
Distribute Writing Assignment #1 in which the students will create a short story based on the cases they researched for their non-fiction assignment. In their stories, they will create a plausible solution to the previously unsolved case based on evidence provided in the articles. These will be written in short story form, preferably in third person omniscient narration.

<u>Activity 4</u>
Prior to your next class meeting, students should preview the study questions for Chapters 7 and 8 and do the related pre-reading vocabulary work. Students should also read Chapters 7 and 8. If students complete the writing assignment with class time remaining, they may use the time to begin this assignment.

# WRITING ASSIGNMENT #1
*And Then There Were None*
Creative Writing

## PROMPT
You have been researching a particular unsolved mystery for your non-fiction reading assignment. You will use the information provided in the articles to create a plausible solution for the crime and then present the case in short story form.

## PREWRITING
Create a story outline using the information you gleaned from the non-fiction articles about a particular unsolved mystery:

*Exposition:* Introduce the characters and the setting of the story
*Rising Action:* What conflicts surround the crime?
*Climax:* The Crime is committed
*Falling Action:* The investigation—everything begins to unravel for the guilty party
*Denouement (Resolution):* The crime is solved and explained

## DRAFTING
Following your prewriting outline, create a short story surrounding the case you researched. Create characters that are believable based on the factual evidence and a plot that follows the details of the case. The climax should include the description of the crime based on police reports, and the falling action should reflect the investigation that was carried out. Your resolution of the crime must be logical, based on the facts…nothing improbable! You are required to correctly use ten vocabulary words from the unit throughout your story.

## PEER CONFERENCING/REVISING
When you finish the rough draft of your paper, ask a student who sits near you to read it. After reading your rough draft, he/she should tell you what he/she liked best about your work, which parts were difficult to understand, and ways in which your work could be improved. Reread your paper considering your critic's comments, and make the corrections you think are necessary.

## PROOFREADING
Do a final proofreading of your paper double-checking your grammar, spelling, organization, and the clarity of your ideas.

# WRITING EVALUATION FORM - *And Then There Were None*

Name _____ Date _____

Grade _____

Circle One For Each Item:

| | | |
|---|---|---|
| Grammar: | correct | errors noted on paper |
| Spelling: | correct | errors noted on paper |
| Punctuation: | correct | errors noted on paper |
| Legibility: | excellent | good    fair    poor |
| | excellent | good    fair    poor |
| | excellent | good    fair    poor |

Strengths:



Weaknesses:



Comments/Suggestions:

# LESSON FIVE

<u>Objectives</u>
1. To review the main events and ideas in Chapters 7 and 8
2. To demonstrate an understanding of characterization through the creation of posters
3. To demonstrate their understanding of the difference between a physical characteristic and a character trait
4. To practice note-taking skills while listening to others' presentations
5. To preview the study questions and do the vocabulary work for Chapters 9 and 10
6. To read Chapters 9 and 10

<u>Activity 1</u>
Discuss the answers to the study questions for Chapters 7 and 8 as previously discussed.

<u>Activity 2</u>
Divide students into 10 pairs/groups for the following: Vera Claythorne, Philip Lombard, Mr. Rogers, Mrs. Rogers, Judge Wargrave, Dr. Armstrong, Mr. Blore, Emily Brent, Anthony Marston, and General Macarthur.

Each pair/group will be given a large sheet of construction paper to be used to create a character poster. On each poster, the groups must provide the following:

* the name of the character

* a labeled picture of the character based on the physical description given in the text (labels should contain page numbers as evidence)

* a list of at least three positive character traits with supporting evidence and corresponding page numbers for each

* a list of at least three negative character traits with supporting evidence and corresponding page numbers for each

* a description of the crime each had been accused of and list of clues surrounding these crimes

<u>Activity 3</u>
After students finish their posters, each pair/group must get up in front of the class and share the information about its particular character. Those who are not presenting must take notes about the other characters. Remind students that they will all be responsible for being able to identify all of the characters on the unit test. When all are finished sharing, allow students to speculate on the guilt or innocence of each character. Who might be the murderer on Indian Island?

<u>Activity 4</u>
Tell students that prior to the next class meeting they should preview the study questions, do the vocabulary work, and complete the reading for Chapters 9 and 10.

# LESSON SIX

<u>Objectives</u>
1. To review the main events and ideas from Chapters 9 and 10
2. To evaluate students' oral reading skills
3. To preview the study questions, do the vocabulary worksheets, and complete the reading for chapters 11 and 12

<u>Activity 1</u>
Discuss the answers to the study questions for Chapters 9 and 10 as previously directed. While students have their study guides out, also preview the questions for Chapters 11 and 12.

<u>Activity 2</u>
Do the vocabulary worksheet for Chapters 11 and 12 together orally in class.

<u>Activity 3</u>
If you have not completed the oral reading evaluations begun in Lesson Two, use this class time to finish them as students read Chapters 11 and 12. If you have completed them, students may use this class period for the independent, silent reading of Chapters 11 and 12. This reading assignment should be completed prior to your next class period.

<u>Activity 4</u>
If students are reading silently and finish reading early, they should review their study questions or vocabulary work--or work on their short stories from Writing Assignment #1.

# LESSON SEVEN

Objectives
1. To review the main events and ideas from Chapters 11 and 12
2. To improve research skills while working in the library/media center
3. To practice writing to inform
4. To preview the study questions, do the vocabulary worksheet, and compete the reading for Chapters 13 and 14

Activity 1
Discuss the answers to the study questions for Chapters 11 and 12 as previously directed. Preview the study questions for Chapters 13 and 14 while students have their study guides out.

Activity 2
Distribute Writing Assignment #2 and discuss the directions in detail. Students will research topics relating to the various characters of the novel. You may either allow students to choose which character topics they would like to research or assign students characters for which they created the character sketches in Lesson Five. Go to the library/media center for the research.

Activity 3
Prior to the next class meeting, students should complete the vocabulary worksheet and do the reading for Chapters 13 and 14. If time remains in this class period, they may begin working on this assignment.

# WRITING ASSIGNMENT #2
*And Then There Were None*
Writing to Inform

PROMPT:
You have been reading Agatha Christie's *And Then There Were None*. Based on events from the past, each character has his/her own reason to be frightened on Indian Island. You are going to be provided with two topics relating to each character and your assignment is to research the general topics and then show how the topics relate to the character from the novel.

PREWRITING:
Select **one** of the following characters with its corresponding topics to research:

**Philip Lombard:**
- Illegal activities for hire
- Permits for carrying firearms (in England)

**Emily Brent:**
- Puritan attitudes about proper behavior befitting ladies and gentlemen
- Religious/Social hypocrisy

**Dr. Armstrong:**
- Increased insurance costs due to malpractice suits
- The influence of alcohol on performing manual tasks (those with the hands)

**Judge Lawrence Wargrave:**
- The chancery court system in Great Britain
- "hanging" judges

**Mr. and Mrs. Rogers:**
- the role of house servants in British society
- care of invalid patients

**Vera Claythorne:**
- The role of the governess in British Society
- Crimes of passion

**Mr. Blore:**
- Cases of perjury
- Corruption in law enforcement

**General Macarthur:**
- WWI reconnaissance missions
- Jealousy as a motivator

**Anthony Marston:**
- Reckless driving
- The wealthy are sometimes not punished as severely as the poor for the same crimes

And Then There Were None Writing Assignment #2 Continued

DRAFTING:
Your introduction should include a character sketch for the person you have selected. Use your character sketch notes (taken during the poster presentations) to help you. For the body, be sure to write at least two paragraphs for each of the subtopics provided based on your research findings: one about the topic in general, and one about how your character relates to the topic. Conclude with whether or not you believe the character is guilty of the crime he/she is charged with. Be sure to provide logical reasons for your decision. You are required to correctly use four vocabulary words from the unit in your essay.

PEER CONFERENCING/REVISING
When you finish the rough draft of your paper, ask a student who sits near you to read it. After reading your rough draft, he/she should tell you what he/she liked best about your work, which parts were difficult to understand, and ways in which your work could be improved. Reread your paper considering your critic's comments, and make the corrections you think are necessary.

PROOFREADING
Do a final proofreading of your paper double-checking your grammar, spelling, organization, and the clarity of your ideas.

# LESSON EIGHT

<u>Objectives</u>
1. To review the main events and ideas from Chapters 13 and 14
2. To practice cooperative learning skills through the completion of a group project (a board game)
3. To preview the study guide questions and vocabulary for chapters 15 and 16
4. To read Chapters 15 and 16

<u>Activity 1</u>
Discuss the answers to the study questions for Chapters 13 and 14 as previously directed. Preview the questions for Chapters 15 and 16 while students have their study guides out.

<u>Activity 2</u>
Divide class into four groups. Each group will then select one of the three following board games and create a version of the game based on *And Then There Were None:*

Clue (the obvious one!)

Trivial Pursuit

A creative "path" game that incorporates questions/facts/characters/setting from the novel

***Be sure that the teams divide the responsibilities for the creation of the game evenly:***

    writing the rules of the game

    making the game board

    creating a decorated box (with title of the game) that will hold all the pieces and the board

    making game cards

    making game pieces that reflect the theme of the game

<u>Activity 3</u>
Let students have the remainder of the class as a brainstorming session. Tell them to bring any supplies that they plan on using from home to Lesson Eleven (that will be a working day to put the games together). Have them generate a list of supplies that will be needed in order to make the game and look over each list. Your Art department might be able to supply some of the necessary materials that the students might need.

<u>Activity 4</u>
Tell students that prior to the next class meeting they should complete the vocabulary worksheet and do the reading for Chapters 15 and 16. If time remains in this class period after students finish brainstorming ideas for the game project, they may use the rest of the class time to work on this assignment.

# LESSON NINE

## Objectives
1. To review the main events and ideas from Chapters 15 and 16
2. To preview the study questions and vocabulary for the Epilogue and the Letter
3. To complete reading *And Then There Were None*

## Activity 1
Discuss the answers to the study questions for Chapters 15 and 16 as previously directed. Preview the study questions for the Epilogue and the Letter.

## Activity 2
Do the vocabulary worksheet for the last reading assignment together orally in class.

## Activity 3
Students should use this class time to complete the last reading assignment. If you have not completed the oral reading evaluations, this is your last chance to do so.

# LESSON TEN

<u>Objectives</u>
1. To review the main ideas and events for the last reading assignment
2. To practice independent working skills through in-class writing (working on the mystery stories)

<u>Activity 1</u>
Discuss the answers to the study questions for the last reading assignment as previously directed.

<u>Activity 2</u>
Give students the remainder of this class period to work on their mystery stories from Writing Assignment #1.

While students are working, you might use this time to individually review students' oral reading evaluations, to circulate through the room helping students with their stories, or to work separately with any students who have already completed the mystery story assignment.

Students who have already completed the mystery story should review their study guides and vocabulary worksheets.

# LESSON ELEVEN

Objectives
1. To practice personal interaction skills through working in cooperative groups
2. To demonstrate comprehension of the novel through creation of a board game

Activity

Students should use this class time to actually create the board games they began to plan in Lesson Eight. Any materials they brought with them can be supplemented by materials previously gleaned from your school's Art department or elsewhere. By the end of this period, the game boards, boxes, cards, pieces, and questions should be completed.

Students who finish early should play their board games. If two groups finish early, they could swap games and play.

# LESSON TWELVE

Objectives
To review the vocabulary work done in this unit

Activity 1
Choose one (or more) of the vocabulary review activities listed below and spend your class period as directed in the activity. Some of the materials for these review activities are located in the Vocabulary Resource Materials section in this LitPlan.

## VOCABULARY REVIEW ACTIVITIES

1. Divide your class into two teams and have an old-fashioned spelling or definition bee.

2. Give each of your students (or students in groups of two, three or four) an *And Then There Were None* Vocabulary Word Search Puzzle. The person (group) to find all of the vocabulary words in the puzzle first wins.

3. Give students an *And Then There Were None* Vocabulary Word Search Puzzle without the word list. The person or group to find the most vocabulary words in the puzzle wins.

4. Use an *And Then There Were None* Vocabulary Crossword Puzzle. Put the puzzle onto a transparency on the overhead projector (so everyone can see it), and do the puzzle together as a class.

5. Give students an *And Then There Were None* Vocabulary Matching Worksheet to do.

6. Divide your class into two teams. Use *And Then There Were None* vocabulary words with their letters jumbled as a word list. Student 1 from Team A faces off against Student 1 from Team B. You write the first jumbled word on the board. The first student (1A or 1B) to unscramble the word wins the chance for his/her team to score points. If 1A wins the jumble, go to student 2A and give him/her a definition. He/she must give you the correct spelling of the vocabulary word which fits that definition. If he/she does, Team A scores a point, and you give student 3A a definition for which you expect a correctly spelled matching vocabulary word. Continue giving Team A definitions until some team member makes an incorrect response. An incorrect response sends the game back to the jumbled-word face off, this time with students 2A and 2B. Instead of repeating giving definitions to the first few students of each team, continue with the student after the one who gave the last incorrect response on the team. For example, if Team B wins the jumbled-word face-off, and student 5B gave the last incorrect answer for Team B, you would start this round of definition questions with student 6B, and so on. The team with the most points wins!

7. Play "I Have... Who Has?" This requires advance preparation, but the students really seem to enjoy it. Using your entire vocabulary list from *And Then There Were None*, create a set of cards where the definition for the first word is written on the first card, but the word that goes WITH the definition is written on the second card. On the BACK of the second card, write the definition for the second word, and on the third card, write the second word... continue until you come to the end of the list. Write the final word on the back of the first card that has definition #1. (The whole set will create an entire loop of vocabulary words). Shuffle the cards and distribute among the students, keeping one for yourself. Have students put the cards on their desks with the word facing UP. You then say, "Who has..." and read the definition on the back of the card. Whichever student who has the card with the correct vocabulary word that

matches the definition calls out, "I have..." and reads the word. He/She then flips that card over and says, "Who has..." and reads the definition. The game continues until the loop returns with the card in the teacher's hand matches the last definition read. Use a stop watch and get various classes try to beat the best times.

8. Have students write a story in which they correctly use as many vocabulary words as possible. Have students read their compositions orally! Post the most original compositions on your bulletin board!

Activity 2
Divide the questions from the Extra Discussion Questions/Writing Assignments (see Lesson Thirteen) among your students, selecting those you feel are most appropriate for your students. Since a class discussion of these questions is most effective if students have been given the opportunity to formulate answers to the questions prior to the discussion, assign specific questions to each student and have them prepare a response for the next class day. To this end, you may either have all the students formulate answers to all the questions, divide your class into groups and assign one or more questions to each group, or you could assign one question to each student in your class. The class discussion of these questions is scheduled for Lesson Thirteen.

NOTE: The use of graphic organizers may be helpful to students in preparing their answers. Encourage them to use any diagrams or graphics that they feel are necessary.

# LESSON THIRTEEN

<u>Objectives</u>
To discuss and demonstrate an understanding of the book on an analytical level

<u>Activity</u>
Have students share their responses to the assigned questions from the Extra Discussion Questions/Writing Assignments (the homework from the previous class). During the discussion of student responses, all students are required to take notes on the questions for the unit test.

# EXTRA WRITING ASSIGNMENTS/DISCUSSION QUESTIONS
*And Then There Were None*

<u>Interpretive</u>

1. Describe the setting of the novel. What particular elements of the setting help create an atmosphere of mystery and suspense?
2. Provide a character sketch for three of the guests of Indian Island. Be sure to explain both negative and positive character traits as well as give a description of the crime that each is accused of committing.
3. Re-examine the conversation between Vera Claythorne and Emily Brent in which Emily Brent claims that she has "nothing with which to reproach [herself]." What does this show about her character? Why does she seem to think she is above reproach for the crime that she has been accused of?
4. Why do you suppose General Macarthur gives in so easily to the idea that the guests will never leave the island and becomes resigned to his fate?
5. As Vera Claythorne was on her way to Indian Island, what "picture rose clearly" in her mind? At first read, why would this event seem to make her sad? After completing the novel, what seems to be the true reason for her sadness?
6. Fully describe the Edward Seton case and how Judge Wargrave had "cooked Seton's goose." What information about Edward Seton was later revealed after the general public had been led to believe that Seton had been innocent? What does this case demonstrate about Judge Wargrave's character?
7. After hearing the accusations made by "the voice" on the record, Rogers drops the coffee tray. What do you suppose is the reason that he loses control of the tray? What does this show about his character?
8. Fully describe Dr. Armstrong's dream that he has after the voice accuses him of murder. What does this dream say about his character?
9. Not much specific information has been given surrounding the activities that Philip Lombard has been involved in. What clues have been dropped that hint that Lombard's activities were not always legitimate? Why does Lombard suppose he was hired to "keep his eyes open" on Indian Island?
10. Explain Wargrave's suicide as he describes it in his letter. How does he manage to make his suicide look like murder? Why does it matter to Wargrave, since he is going to be dead, that his death must look like murder?

Critical

1. How does the author's use of the nursery rhyme throughout the novel add to the creation of suspense?
2. While on the train, Mr. Blore meets an old man who tells him to "watch and pray. The day of judgment is at hand." How does this statement foreshadow the events on Indian Island?
3. Speculate on the psychological influence of a guilty conscience. How does that idea seem to fit in with the events on Indian Island? Select two characters who seem to be especially influenced by a guilty conscience and explain how it affects the characters' behavior.
4. What psychological impact does the disappearance of the china figurines seem to have on the characters in the novel? Why might they react as they do?
5. Explain General Macarthur's motive for sending Arthur Richmond on a reconnaissance mission knowing that he would not return alive.
6. Explain why Vera Claythorne allowed Cyril to swim out to the rock that day on the beach. What was her true motive?
7. Notice how the guests go from being served a sumptuous dinner upon their arrival at Indian Island to eating cold tinned tongue while standing in the kitchen to not wanting to eat at all. How does this progression mirror the events of the island?
8. At several points throughout the novel, the guests are compared to various animals. How does each character seem to reflect specific traits about the animal it is linked to? How is the link to animals symbolic of the state of affairs on the island?
9. From whose point of view is this story told? How does this type of narration affect the overall mood of the novel? How does it help create suspense?
10. Examine the order in which the deaths occurred and the victims' degree of guilt of the crimes they had been accused of. Based on what you have learned about each of the characters, is it appropriate that Vera is the last to die? Why? What is most effective about the method of her demise?

Critical/Personal Response

1. Suppose that Edward Seton was truly innocent as the general public believed. How would that fact change your view of Judge Wargrave and the outline of his scheme for punishing those guilty parties who were unable to be punished by the law?
2. Suppose Dr. Armstrong had decided not to help Judge Wargrave fake his death. How might the story have changed?
3. Suppose Vera had not hanged herself at the end of the novel. What do you think might have happened then?
4. Did you have any sympathy for any of the characters in the novel? Which one(s)? Why or why not?
5. This particular murder mystery is different from most in that there is no detective to solve the crime. How does that fact affect your enjoyment of the novel?

Personal Response

1. What might you have done if you had been placed in a similar situation on an island. What steps might you have taken to survive?
2. If you were to be cast in a movie or stage version of the novel, which character would you most like to portray? Why?
3. Which character would you least like to play in a screen or stage version of the novel? Why?
4. Have you ever been called on something you have done wrong only to deny doing it? How did it make you feel knowing that someone else knew the truth?
5. Have you ever felt guilty for doing something you knew was wrong and you never told anyone? How did it affect the way you behaved in certain situations that reminded you of the incident?
6. Have you ever told anyone about something you did wrong that you felt bad about? How did it feel to tell someone? What suggestions did he/she make to help you feel better?

# LESSON FOURTEEN

<u>Objectives</u>
1. To practice interpersonal skills through playing the games created by classmates
2. To review through playing games related to the novel

<u>Activity</u>
Have students break into their four groups. Each group will take turns playing the various board games created by their classmates. The questions in the games will help students review important characters, events, and ideas from the novel.

# LESSON FIFTEEN

<u>Objectives</u>
1. To demonstrate writing skills through the completion of an in-class writing assignment
2. To evaluate students' writing skills
3. To practice and demonstrate the ability to persuade

<u>Activity</u>
Distribute Writing Assignment #3 and discuss the directions in detail. Give students ample time to complete the assignment in class.

If students finish early, they may study for the test or work on editing their mystery stories (if they have not completed them yet).

# WRITING ASSIGNMENT #3
*And Then There Were None*
Persuasive: Guilty or Not Guilty?

PROMPT
You have finished reading murder mystery *And Then There Were None*. In this novel, Judge Lawrence Wargrave takes the law into his own hands to punish those guilty persons who were not able to be punished by the law under due process. You must decide whether Wargrave was actually committing cold-blooded murder or whether he merely carrying out justice.

PREWRITING
You must describe the reason that Wargrave gives for concocting his plot. Make a chart of pros and cons for each character involved in Wargrave's plot depending on whether each deserved the death penalty for his/her crime. Each pro and con must be evidence from the text as support for your argument.

DRAFTING
Introduce your topic in the first paragraph, being sure to end with a thesis statement. The introduction should introduce Judge Wargrave's reason for concocting his plot and your thesis should mention your position regarding his actions. In your body paragraphs, you must give two specific reasons to support your decision. These will be your first two body paragraphs. Don't forget to embed quotations from the text as evidence for your argument. Your next two body paragraphs will explain why the opposite position is unsound. Again, you must present textual evidence for support. Be sure to incorporate at least four vocabulary words from the unit into your essay. End the conclusion by challenging your reader in some way.

PEER CONFERENCE/REVISING
When you finish the draft, ask another student to look at it. You may want to give the student your pre-writing notes and scenario so he/she can double check to see you have included all the information you intended to include. After reading, he/she should tell you what is best about your essay, which parts were difficult to understand or follow, and ways in which your essay could be improved. Reread your essay considering your critic's comments and make the corrections you think are necessary. You will be completing a peer editing form the next class.

PROOFREADING/EDITING
Do a final proofreading of your essay, double-checking your grammar, spelling, organization, and the clarity of your ideas.

# LESSON SIXTEEN

Objectives
1. To demonstrate and practice editing skills
2. To demonstrate and practice the ability to accept constructive criticism and discern which of the criticism should be acted upon

Activity 1
Put students in pairs for peer editing and give each student a peer evaluation form. Students will exchange their persuasive essays written in class the day before and make comments regarding content, language use, and conventions (under "Editor"). Students will return the essays to the writer and then they respond to their peers' comments about their own writing on the editing sheet (under "Writer"). After thanking his/her peer for their comments, the writer will revise and rewrite the essay to turn in for a grade.

Activity 2
After students have edited and revised their writing and have turned their essays in to be graded, they may work on finishing their projects for the upcoming presentations.

Editor's Name _____  Date _____

Writer's Name _____ Assignment _____

## Peer Editing for Writing Assignments

**A. Was the writer's position clearly stated?**

*If your answer is "yes," be sure to tell the writer what he/she did that you especially liked. If your answer is "no," tell the writer what he/she could have included in order to write a better essay.*

*Editor:* _____
_____
_____

*Writer:* _____
_____
_____

**B. Did he/she provide enough details to support his/her position?**

*If your answer is "yes," be sure to tell the writer what you especially liked about his/her response. If your answer is "no," you must tell the writer how he/she could improve his/her response (adding specific details that were missed, connecting to position better, or adding embedded quotations).*

*Editor:* _____
_____
_____

*Writer:* _____
_____
_____

**C. Identify sentence type**

*Be sure to know the difference between simple, simple with compound subject, simple with compound predicate, compound, complex, and compound-complex. Using the first body paragraph, correctly identify each sentence type. If there is sufficient sentence structure variety, tell the writer what he/she did well. If not, explain what he/she could have done differently.*

*Sentence 1:* _____   *Sentence 5:* _____

*Sentence 2:* _____   *Sentence 6:* _____

*Sentence 3:* _____   *Sentence 7:* _____

*Sentence 4:* _____   *Sentence 8:* _____

*Editor:*_____
_____
_____

*Writer:*_____
_____
_____

### D. Address the Focus Correction Areas
*Did the writer follow the specifics of the essay such as (address each individually):*

**Organization:**

*Editor:* _____

*Writer:* _____

**Use of Vocabulary as Directed:**

*Editor:* _____

*Writer:* _____

**Citations from novel as support:**

*Editor:* _____

*Writer:* _____

### E. Check for Errors in Punctuation, Grammar, Spelling, etc.

*Editor:* _____

*Writer:* _____

**Comments:**

# LESSONS SEVENTEEN AND EIGHTEEN

<u>Objectives</u>
1. To practice public speaking skills
2. To practice listening skills
3. To practice reasoning skills
4. To let students show off their work to their peers and get feedback

<u>Activity</u>
Have students take turns reading their mystery stories aloud. Ask each student to stop briefly before revealing the guilty party and take a poll of the class to see if they can guess the guilty party--and explain their reasoning. Then have the author finish reading his/her story. Make these fun days for students! Take a quick (unannounced) poll to vote on the best story and give a little prize.

# LESSON NINETEEN

Objectives
To review the ideas and events from the entire novel in preparation for the unit test

Activity
Choose one of the review games or activities below and spend your class time as directed. You may choose to use several of these activities.

## REVIEW GAMES AND ACTIVITIES

1. Ask the class to make up a unit test for *And Then There Were None*. The test should have 4 sections: matching, true/false, short answer, and essay. Students may use half the class period to make the test and then swap papers and use the other half of the class period to take a test a classmate has devised. (open book) You may want to use the unit test included in this packet or take questions from the students' unit tests to formulate your own test.

2. Take half of the class period for students to make up true and false questions (including the answers). Collect the papers and divide the class into two teams. Draw a big tic-tac-toe board on the chalk board. Make one team X and one team O. Ask questions to each side, giving each student one turn. If the question is answered correctly, that students' team's letter (X or O) is placed in the box. If the answer is incorrect, no letter is placed in the box. The object is to get three in a row like tic-tac-toe. You may want to keep track of the number of games won for each team.

3. Take half of the class period for students to make up questions (true/false and short answer). Collect the questions. Divide the class into two teams. You'll alternate asking questions to individual members of teams A & B (like in a spelling bee). The question keeps going from A to B until it is correctly answered, then a new question is asked. A correct answer does not allow the team to get another question. Correct answers are +2 points; incorrect answers are -1 point.

4. Have students pair up and quiz each other from their study guides and class notes.

5. Give students an *And Then There Were None* crossword puzzle to complete.

6. Divide your class into two teams. Use *And Then There Were None* crossword words with their letters jumbled as a word list. Student 1 from Team A faces off against Student 1 from Team B. You write the first jumbled word on the board. The first student (1A or 1B) to unscramble the word wins the chance for his/her team to score points. If 1A wins the jumble, go to student 2A and give him/her a clue. He/she must give you the correct word which matches that clue. If he/she does, Team A scores a point, and you give student 3A a clue for which you expect another correct response. Continue giving Team A clues until some team member makes an incorrect response. An incorrect response sends the game back to the jumbled-word face off, this time with students 2A and 2B. Instead of repeating giving clues to the first few students of each team, continue with the student after the one who gave the last incorrect response on the team. For example, if Team B wins the jumbled-word face-off, and student 5B gave the last incorrect answer for Team B, you would start this round of clue questions with student 6B, and so on. The team with the most points wins!

7. Play *What's My Line?*. This is similar to the old television show. Students assume the roles of different characters from the novel. One student gives clues to the class, or to a panel of

contestants. The contestants try to guess the identity of the guest. Students may enjoy assisting you in creating rules and procedures for the game.

8. Play Jeopardy. Divide the class into two groups. Assign each group a category or book from the novel and have them devise answers for that category. Play the game according to the television show procedures.

9. Play Drawing in the Details. This is similar to Pictionary. Divide students into teams. A student from one team draws a scene from the text. Drawings should be kept simple, to keep the pace lively. Students in the opposing team locate the scene in their books and read it aloud. If they are incorrect, the illustrator's team has a chance to guess. Involve students in setting up a scoring system and any other necessary rules.

# LESSON TWENTY

<u>Objectives</u>
To assess students' understanding of the main ideas and events presented in Agatha Christie's *And Then There Were None*

<u>Activity</u>
Distribute the unit tests, give students ample time to complete them, and collect the tests when students finish. Remember to collect assigned books prior to the end of the class period.

NOTE: There are 5 different unit tests included in this LitPlan Teacher Pack. Two are short answer, two are multiple choice. There is one advanced short answer test. The answers to the short answer tests will be based on the discussions you have had during class and should be graded accordingly. You should choose the tests and/or test parts which best suit your needs. Matching and short answer tests have answer keys. For essay type questions, grade according to your own criteria based on class discussions and the level of your students. Also, you will need to choose vocabulary words to read orally for the vocabulary sections of the short answer tests.

# UNIT TESTS

*And Then There Were None* Short Answer Unit Test 1

I. Matching I

____ 1. ROGERS     A. Killed someone for sleeping with his wife
____ 2. VERA       B. Run down by a reckless driver
____ 3. MARSTON    C. Conducted the purchase of Indian Island for an unnamed third party
____ 4. MACARTHUR  D. Drowned herself after becoming pregnant
____ 5. EMILY      E. Killed an employer by withholding medicine
____ 6. BRENT      F. Mr. Blore's assumed name when he arrived on the island
____ 7. LOMBARD    G. Knew that murder had been committed in order to win his love
____ 8. BLORE      H. Had an affair with his friend's wife
____ 9. WARGRAVE   I. The supposed owner of the island: Mr. U. N. ____
____ 10. BEATRICE  J. Captain of the boat that took the guests to Indian Island
____ 11. ARTHUR    K. Killed someone by being too reckless
____ 12. HUGO      L. Emily's last name
____ 13. CYRIL     M. Famous for making harsh judgments
____ 14. MORRIS    N. Died after necessary medicine was withheld
____ 15. NARRACOTT O. Committed perjury which led to the death of an innocent man
____ 16. DAVIS     P. Led someone to suicide through moral judgment
____ 17. OWEN      Q. Abandoned a group of men under attack
____ 18. CLEES     R. Drowned when allowed to swim too far out to sea
____ 19. COMBES    S. Died on the operating table
____ 20. BRADY     T. Allowed a weak young boy to drown

II. Short Answer

1. What is in the center of the dining room table?

2. What hangs above the mantelpiece in each of the bedrooms in the island mansion?

3. What reason does Emily Brent give for coming to Indian Island?

4. Who is the one person who refuses to speak about the charges made against him/her?

5. Why doesn't Lombard believe that Mrs. Rogers killed herself?

6. After their search, what do Blore, Armstrong, and Lombard discover about the island?

7. Why had the people of Sticklehaven not attempted to make contact with anyone on Indian Island?

8. How do the police manage to solve the crime of Indian Island?

9. How did the killer manage to complete the scheme without getting caught by the others?

III. Complete Answer
1. Provide a character sketch for three of the guests of Indian Island. Be sure to explain both negative and positive character traits as well as give a description of the crime that each is accused of committing.

2. How does the author's use of the nursery rhyme throughout the novel add to the creation of suspense?

3. From whose point of view is this story told? How does this type of narration affect the overall mood of the novel? How does it help create suspense?

4. Examine the order in which the deaths occurred and the victims' degree of guilt of the crimes they had been accused of. Based on what you have learned about each of the characters, is it appropriate that Vera is the last to die? Why? What is most effective about the method of her demise?

IV. Vocabulary
   A. Write the vocabulary words you are given. After writing them down, go back and write in their definitions.

| Word | Definition |
|---|---|
| 1 | |
| 2 | |
| 3 | |
| 4 | |
| 5 | |
| 6 | |
| 7 | |
| 8 | |
| 9 | |
| 10 | |

*And Then There Were None* Short Answer Unit Test 1 Answer Key

I. Matching I

| | | | | | |
|---|---|---|---|---|---|
| E | 1. | ROGERS | A. | Killed someone for sleeping with his wife |
| T | 2. | VERA | B. | Run down by a reckless driver |
| K | 3. | MARSTON | C. | Conducted the purchase of Indian Island for an unnamed third party |
| A | 4. | MACARTHUR | D. | Drowned herself after becoming pregnant |
| P | 5. | EMILY | E. | Killed an employer by withholding medicine |
| L | 6. | BRENT | F. | Mr. Blore's assumed name when he arrived on the island |
| Q | 7. | LOMBARD | G. | Knew that murder had been committed in order to win his love |
| O | 8. | BLORE | H. | Had an affair with his friend's wife |
| M | 9. | WARGRAVE | I. | The supposed owner of the island: Mr. U. N. ___ |
| D | 10. | BEATRICE | J. | Captain of the boat that took the guests to Indian Island |
| H | 11. | ARTHUR | K. | Killed someone by being too reckless |
| G | 12. | HUGO | L. | Emily's last name |
| R | 13. | CYRIL | M. | Famous for making harsh judgments |
| C | 14. | MORRIS | N. | Died after necessary medicine was withheld |
| J | 15. | NARRACOTT | O. | Committed perjury which led to the death of an innocent man |
| F | 16. | DAVIS | P. | Led someone to suicide through moral judgment |
| I | 17. | OWEN | Q. | Abandoned a group of men under attack |
| S | 18. | CLEES | R. | Drowned when allowed to swim too far out to sea |
| B | 19. | COMBES | S. | Died on the operating table |
| N | 20. | BRADY | T. | Allowed a weak young boy to drown |

II. Short Answer
1. What is in the center of the dining room table?
   *Ten china figures of little Indian boys are set in a circle in the center of the dining room table.*

2. What hangs above the mantelpiece in each of the bedrooms in the island mansion?
   *A framed verse, "The Little Indian Boys," hangs over the mantelpieces of each bedroom in the island mansion.*

3. What reason does Emily Brent give for coming to Indian Island?
   *She received an invitation to join a friend she'd met two summers ago for a holiday at Indian Island.*

4. Who is the one person who refuses to speak about the charges made against him/her?
   *Emily Brent refuses to speak about the charges made against her.*

5. Why doesn't Lombard believe that Mrs. Rogers killed herself?
   *Lombard believes that it is too much of a coincidence for two suicides to occur within such a short time period.*

6. After their search, what do Blore, Armstrong, and Lombard discover about the island?
   *They discovered there is no place to hide on the island except for inside the house.*

7. Why had the people of Sticklehaven not attempted to make contact with anyone on Indian Island?
   *Mr. Morris had told the townsfolk that Mr. Owen was hosting a contest about who could best survive on a desert island for a week and that no one from the town could interfere.*

8. How do the police manage to solve the crime of Indian Island?
   *A fisherman finds a confession in a sealed bottle floating in the water.*

9. How did the killer manage to complete the scheme without getting caught by the others?
   *Wargrave faked his death with the help of Dr. Armstrong. He got him to go along with it by telling the doctor that he could watch over the group and ferret out the killer if everyone thought he was dead. Wargrave later pushed his accomplice off a cliff.*

IV. Vocabulary
    A. Write the vocabulary words you are given. After writing them down, go back and write in their definitions.

| Word | Definition |
|---|---|
| 1 | |
| 2 | |
| 3 | |
| 4 | |
| 5 | |
| 6 | |
| 7 | |
| 8 | |
| 9 | |
| 10 | |

Select the vocabulary words for Short Answer Test 1

*And Then There Were None* Short Answer Unit Test 2

I. Matching

____ 1.  ROGERS        A. Died after necessary medicine was withheld

____ 2.  VERA          B. Abandoned a group of men under attack

____ 3.  MARSTON       C. Wargrave's occupation

____ 4.  MACARTHUR     D. Killed an employer by withholding medicine

____ 5.  EMILY         E. Had an affair with his friend's wife

____ 6.  LOMBARD       F. The supposed owner of the island: Mr. U. N. ___

____ 7.  BLORE         G. Died on the operating table

____ 8.  JUDGE         H. Wargrave "cooked HIS goose."

____ 9.  TAYLOR        I. Led someone to suicide through moral judgment

____ 10. ARTHUR        J. Beatrice's last name

____ 11. HUGO          K. Committed perjury which led to the death of an innocent man

____ 12. CYRIL         L. Conducted the purchase of Indian Island for an unnamed third party

____ 13. MORRIS        M. Allowed a weak young boy to drown

____ 14. NARRACOTT     N. Drowned when allowed to swim too far out to sea

____ 15. DAVIS         O. Captain of the boat that took the guests to Indian Island

____ 16. OWEN          P. Knew that murder had been committed in order to win his love

____ 17. CLEES         Q. Killed someone for sleeping with his wife

____ 18. BRADY         R. Mr. Blore's assumed name when he arrived on the island

____ 19. SETON         S. Killed someone by being too reckless

____ 20. CHRISTIE      T. Author of *And Then There Were None*

II. Short Answer

1. What warning does Blore receive from the old man on the train?

2. What is in the center of the dining room table?

3. What conclusion does Wargrave come to about the owner of the house?

4. What conclusion does General Macarthur make about their being lured to the island?

5. What does Emily Brent suspect about Mr. and Mrs. Rogers?

6. Which of the characters has accepted his/her fate and waits patiently for the final outcome?

7. After searching the entire house, what do Armstrong, Blore, and Lombard conclude?

8. What does Mr. Lombard find missing from his bed-table?

9. Vera goes to her room to bathe her aching head and temples in cold water. What causes her screams of terror?

10. What does Vera see in her room that she had not noticed before?

11. How does Lombard suggest the survivors make contact with people on the mainland?

12. Who does Vera believe is waiting for her in her bedroom?

13. What does the Assistant Commissioner of Scotland Yard find on Indian Island?

14. Why had the people of Sticklehaven not attempted to make contact with anyone on Indian Island?

15. What makes the inspector absolutely certain that Vera Claythorne had not committed the murders?

16. How do the police manage to solve the crime of Indian Island?




17. Who was the murderer on Indian Island?




18. Why did the murderer decide on these particular ten victims?

III. Complete Answer
1. Describe the setting of the novel. What particular elements of the setting help create an atmosphere of mystery and suspense?

2. Speculate on the psychological influence of a guilty conscience. How does that idea seem to fit in with the events on Indian Island? Select two characters who seem to be especially influenced by a guilty conscience and explain how it affects the characters' behavior.

3. From whose point of view is this story told? How does this type of narration affect the overall mood of the novel? How does it help create suspense?

4. What is it about this book that makes it one of the most read, most loved murder mysteries of all time? Choose at least three reasons and support them fully with examples and evidence from the text.

IV. Vocabulary
   A. Write the vocabulary words you are given. After writing them down, go back and write in their definitions.

| Word | Definition |
|---|---|
| 1 | |
| 2 | |
| 3 | |
| 4 | |
| 5 | |
| 6 | |
| 7 | |
| 8 | |
| 9 | |
| 10 | |

*And Then There Were None* Short Answer Unit Test 2 Answer Key

I. Matching

| | | | | |
|---|---|---|---|---|
| D | 1. | ROGERS | A. | Died after necessary medicine was withheld |
| M | 2. | VERA | B. | Abandoned a group of men under attack |
| S | 3. | MARSTON | C. | Wargrave's occupation |
| Q | 4. | MACARTHUR | D. | Killed an employer by withholding medicine |
| I | 5. | EMILY | E. | Had an affair with his friend's wife |
| B | 6. | LOMBARD | F. | The supposed owner of the island: Mr. U. N. ___ |
| K | 7. | BLORE | G. | Died on the operating table |
| C | 8. | JUDGE | H. | Wargrave "cooked HIS goose." |
| J | 9. | TAYLOR | I. | Led someone to suicide through moral judgment |
| E | 10. | ARTHUR | J. | Beatrice's last name |
| P | 11. | HUGO | K. | Committed perjury which led to the death of an innocent man |
| N | 12. | CYRIL | L. | Conducted the purchase of Indian Island for an unnamed third party |
| L | 13. | MORRIS | M. | Allowed a weak young boy to drown |
| O | 14. | NARRACOTT | N. | Drowned when allowed to swim too far out to sea |
| R | 15. | DAVIS | O. | Captain of the boat that took the guests to Indian Island |
| F | 16. | OWEN | P. | Knew that murder had been committed in order to win his love |
| G | 17. | CLEES | Q. | Killed someone for sleeping with his wife |
| A | 18. | BRADY | R. | Mr. Blore's assumed name when he arrived on the island |
| H | 19. | SETON | S. | Killed someone by being too reckless |
| T | 20. | CHRISTIE | T. | Author of *And Then There Were None* |

II. Short Answer

1. What warning does Blore receive from the old man on the train?
   *The old man tells him that the day of judgment is very close at hand.*

2. What is in the center of the dining room table?
   *Ten china figures of little Indian boys are set in a circle in the center of the dining room table.*

3. What conclusion does Wargrave come to about the owner of the house?
   *Both the initials of the owner and his wife were U. N. with the last name Owen. Wargrave concludes that U.N. Owen is an unknown person who has lured them all to the island.*

4. What conclusion does General Macarthur make about their being lured to the island?
   *General Macarthur is sure they will never leave the island.*

5. What does Emily Brent suspect about Mr. and Mrs. Rogers?
   *Emily suspects that the story of them killing their employer for the legacy is true.*

6. Which of the characters has accepted his/her fate and waits patiently for the final outcome?
   *General Macarthur has admitted his guilt and accepts his fate.*

7. After searching the entire house, what do Armstrong, Blore, and Lombard conclude?
   *They conclude there is no one on the island except for the eight remaining guests.*

8. What does Mr. Lombard find missing from his bed-table?
   *His revolver is missing.*

9. Vera goes to her room to bathe her aching head and temples in cold water. What causes her screams of terror?
   *Someone has hung seaweed from a hook on the ceiling of her room, and she walks into it thinking the seaweed is a cold, damp hand.*

10. What does Vera see in her room that she had not noticed before?
    *She sees a large hook in the ceiling near her bed.*

11. How does Lombard suggest the survivors make contact with people on the mainland?
    *He is going to use a mirror to heliograph an S O S to the mainland.*

12. Who does Vera believe is waiting for her in her bedroom?
    *She thinks Hugo is waiting for her in her bedroom.*

13. What does the Assistant Commissioner of Scotland Yard find on Indian Island?
    *He finds ten dead bodies and not a living soul on the island.*

14. Why had the people of Sticklehaven not attempted to make contact with anyone on Indian Island?
    *Mr. Morris had told the townsfolk that Mr. Owen was hosting a contest about who could best survive on a desert island for a week and that no one from the town could interfere.*

15. What makes the inspector absolutely certain that Vera Claythorne had not committed the murders?
    *Although she hanged herself, the chair she had stood on was placed neatly back by the wall by someone else after her death.*

16. How do the police manage to solve the crime of Indian Island?
    *A fisherman finds a confession in a sealed bottle floating in the water.*

17. Who was the murderer on Indian Island?
    *The murderer was Judge Lawrence Wargrave.*

18. Why did the murderer decide on these particular ten victims?
    *All were guilty of murder, yet the law could not touch them.*

IV. Vocabulary
   A. Write the vocabulary words you are given. After writing them down, go back and write in their definitions.

| Word | Definition |
|---|---|
| 1 | |
| 2 | |
| 3 | |
| 4 | |
| 5 | |
| 6 | |
| 7 | |
| 8 | |
| 9 | |
| 10 | |

Select the vocabulary words for Short Answer Test 2

*And Then There Were None* Advanced Short Answer Unit Test

I. Matching

| | | | |
|---|---|---|---|
| ____ 1. | CLAYTHORNE | A. | Author of *And Then There Were None* |
| ____ 2. | MARSTON | B. | Wargrave "cooked HIS goose." |
| ____ 3. | EMILY | C. | Mr. Blore's assumed name when he arrived on the island |
| ____ 4. | PHILLIP | D. | Led someone to suicide through moral judgment |
| ____ 5. | WARGRAVE | E. | Captain of the boat that took the guests to Indian Island |
| ____ 6. | BEATRICE | F. | Mr. Lombard's first name |
| ____ 7. | HUGO | G. | Credited as inventor of the murder mystery genre |
| ____ 8. | CYRIL | H. | Killed someone by being too reckless |
| ____ 9. | NARRACOTT | I. | Drowned herself after becoming pregnant |
| ____ 10. | DAVIS | J. | Run down by a reckless driver |
| ____ 11. | COMBES | K. | Drowned when allowed to swim too far out to sea |
| ____ 12. | BRADY | L. | Died after necessary medicine was withheld |
| ____ 13. | POE | M. | Vera's last name |
| ____ 14. | SETON | N. | Famous for making harsh judgments |
| ____ 15. | CHRISTIE | O. | Knew that murder had been committed in order to win his love |

II. Short Answer
1. Describe the setting of the novel.  What particular elements of the setting help create an atmosphere of mystery and suspense?

2. Why do you suppose General Macarthur gives in so easily to the idea that the guests will never leave the island and becomes resigned to his fate?

3. Explain Wargrave's suicide as he describes it in his letter. How does he manage to make his suicide look like murder? Why does it matter to Wargrave, since he is going to be dead, that his death must look like murder?

4. Explain why Vera Claythorne allowed Cyril to swim out to the rock that day on the beach. What was her true motive?

5. From whose point of view is this story told? How does this type of narration affect the overall mood of the novel? How does it help create suspense?

6. Where is the climax of the story? Justify your answer with evidence from the text.

III. Complete Essay
1. Choose any two characters and compare and contrast the way they reacted to and dealt with the situation.

2. Did all of the "guests" deserve to die? If so, explain why. If not, who did not? Why not?

IV. Vocabulary
   A. Write the vocabulary words you are given. After writing them down, go back and write in their definitions.

| Word | Definition |
|---|---|
| 1 | |
| 2 | |
| 3 | |
| 4 | |
| 5 | |
| 6 | |
| 7 | |
| 8 | |
| 9 | |
| 10 | |

   B. Write a short paragraph using 8 of these 10 words.

*And Then There Were None* Advanced Short Answer Unit Test Answer Key

I. Matching

| | | | | |
|---|---|---|---|---|
| M | 1. | CLAYTHORNE | A. | Author of *And Then There Were None* |
| H | 2. | MARSTON | B. | Wargrave "cooked HIS goose." |
| D | 3. | EMILY | C. | Mr. Blore's assumed name when he arrived on the island |
| F | 4. | PHILLIP | D. | Led someone to suicide through moral judgment |
| N | 5. | WARGRAVE | E. | Captain of the boat that took the guests to Indian Island |
| I | 6. | BEATRICE | F. | Mr. Lombard's first name |
| O | 7. | HUGO | G. | Credited as inventor of the murder mystery genre |
| K | 8. | CYRIL | H. | Killed someone by being too reckless |
| E | 9. | NARRACOTT | I. | Drowned herself after becoming pregnant |
| C | 10. | DAVIS | J. | Run down by a reckless driver |
| J | 11. | COMBES | K. | Drowned when allowed to swim too far out to sea |
| L | 12. | BRADY | L. | Died after necessary medicine was withheld |
| G | 13. | POE | M. | Vera's last name |
| B | 14. | SETON | N. | Famous for making harsh judgments |
| A | 15. | CHRISTIE | O. | Knew that murder had been committed in order to win his love |

IV. Vocabulary
　　A. Write the vocabulary words you are given. After writing them down, go back and write in their definitions.

| Word | Definition |
|---|---|
| 1 | |
| 2 | |
| 3 | |
| 4 | |
| 5 | |
| 6 | |
| 7 | |
| 8 | |
| 9 | |
| 10 | |

　　B. Write a short paragraph using 8 of these 10 words.

Select the vocabulary words for the Advanced Short Answer Test

*And Then There Were None* Multiple Choice Unit Test 1

I. Matching

____ 1. VERA          A. Philip Lombard brought this weapon to the island.

____ 2. MARSTON       B. Vera's hired position with Mrs. Owen

____ 3. EMILY         C. Rogers was killed with this.

____ 4. BLORE         D. Emily noticed one on the dining room window.

____ 5. TAYLOR        E. Killed someone by being too reckless

____ 6. CYRIL         F. Marston's cause of death

____ 7. DAVIS         G. Led someone to suicide through moral judgment

____ 8. BRADY         H. Committed perjury which led to the death of an innocent man

____ 9. REVOLVER      I. Author of *And Then There Were None*

____ 10. INDIAN       J. False clue in a murder mystery: a red ___

____ 11. BOAT         K. Allowed a weak young boy to drown

____ 12. SECRETARY    L. Emily was missing it, and it turned up on the judge.

____ 13. BUTLER       M. Emily's pastime

____ 14. BEACH        N. Job of Mr. Rogers

____ 15. CLOCK        O. This curtain was missing from the bathroom.

____ 16. AXE          P. Where Armstrong's body was found

____ 17. POISON       Q. Vera's means of death

____ 18. HANGING      R. Drowned when allowed to swim too far out to sea

____ 19. YARN         S. Mr. Blore's assumed name when he arrived on the island

____ 20. HERRING      T. The guests anxiously awaited its arrival, but it never came.

____ 21. MURDER       U. Blore was killed with this item.

____ 22. KNITTING     V. Beatrice's last name

____ 23. OILSILK      W. Ten of these figures were on the table in the beginning.

____ 24. BEE          X. The "voice" accused each of the guests of this.

____ 25. CHRISTIE     Y. Died after necessary medicine was withheld

II. Multiple Choice

1. Why is Vera Claythorne going to Indian Island?
    A. She is to serve as temporary secretary to Mrs. Owen.
    B. She is getting married on the island.
    C. She is meeting old friends for a holiday.
    D. She is the new cook for Mrs. Owen.

2. What warning does Blore receive from the old man on the train?
    A. He'd better be properly dressed for the upcoming storm.
    B. The old man tells him to stay away from Indian Island.
    C. The old man tells him that the day of judgment is very close at hand.
    D. The old man tells Blore that someone is out to kill him.

3. What hangs above the mantelpiece in each of the bedrooms in the island mansion?
    A. A seascape
    B. A framed nursery rhyme
    C. A map of the island
    D. A gruesome picture of Mr. U.N. Owen

4. What reason does Emily Brent give for coming to Indian Island?
    A. One of her former students had recommended the Island as a wonderful vacation spot.
    B. Her doctor told her that a vacation by the sea would be good for her poor health.
    C. She is hired as the new cook on Indian Island.
    D. She said she is meeting an old friend who had invited her for a holiday.

5. Of what crime does the "voice" accuse each person in the house?
    A. Arson
    B. Adultery
    C. Murder
    D. Extortion

6. What accusation is made against Wargrave?
    A. He sentenced an innocent man to death.
    B. He killed his wife in a jealous rage.
    C. He killed his employer for a legacy left in her will.
    D. He ran over some children while speeding in his car.

7. What discovery does Rogers make when he goes to clear the dinner dishes from the dining room?
    A. He finds all the dishes in the dining room smashed.
    B. He notices that someone has left the window open.
    C. He notices that one of the china figures is missing.
    D. He finds a small empty vial lying on the floor.

8. What does Emily Brent suspect about Mr. and Mrs. Rogers?
    A. She suspects that they will attempt to leave the island, abandoning the group.
    B. She suspects that they killed their employer for the legacy.
    C. She suspects that they are slowly poisoning the guests with the meals.
    D. She suspects that they are in league with Mr. Owen to destroy them.

9. Why doesn't Lombard believe that Mrs. Rogers killed herself?
    A. She was already nearly unconscious when she was put under a sedative.
    B. She did not have the courage to go through with something like that.
    C. She could not have injected herself with the syringe because she was hysterical.
    D. It is too soon after the death of Tony Marston to be a second suicide.

10. After searching the entire house, what do Armstrong, Blore, and Lombard conclude?
    A. There is no one on the island but the occupants of the house.
    B. There is no murderer; the two deaths must have been suicides after all.
    C. The murderer must have left using the steps carved into the cliff.
    D. The murderer must be hiding in the cave on the south side of the island.

11. Whose name does Emily Brent write in her diary as the murderer?
    A. Dr. Armstrong
    B. Philip Lombard
    C. Beatrice Taylor
    D. Vera Claythorne

12. What does Blore confess to Lombard?
    A. He was hired to make sure no one leaves the island.
    B. He killed General Macarthur.
    C. He is Mr. Owen.
    D. He perjured himself and put an innocent man in prison where the man later died.

13. Emily Brent dreams of Beatrice Taylor. What is Beatrice doing in the dream?
    A. Beatrice is killing Hugo.
    B. Beatrice is pressing her face against the window and moaning, asking to be let in.
    C. Beatrice is laughing at Emily.
    D. Beatrice is throwing her baby into the sea.

14. Who immediately falls under suspicion for Emily's murder?
    A. Dr. Armstrong
    B. Vera
    C. Mr. Blore
    D. Judge Wargrave

15. When Mr. Justice Wargrave is discovered dead what is strange about his appearance?
    A. He is dressed like a General.
    B. He appears to be sleeping.
    C. He is holding the missing revolver.
    D. He is dressed as a judge with a grey wig (the missing yarn) and a scarlet "robe" (the missing oilsilk).

16. How does Lombard suggest the survivors make contact with people on the mainland?
    A. He thinks they could build a signal fire when the rain stops.
    B. He suggests using the telephone, but it is disconnected.
    C. He suggests using a mirror to heliograph an S O S.
    D. He suggests standing on the beach waving white clothing as flags.

17. Vera believes someone is waiting for her in her bedroom. Who?
    A. Philip
    B. Cyril
    C. Hugo
    D. Isaac Morris

18. Why had the people of Sticklehaven not attempted to make contact with anyone on Indian Island?
    A. The storm had made all communication impossible, even though they tried.
    B. They didn't know the owner, so they didn't bother.
    C. They hadn't noticed anything peculiar going on, so they didn't even think about the island.
    D. Mr. Morris told them that there was a contest on the island and to ignore all signals.

19. Why did the murderer decide on these particular ten victims?
    A. They had all come before him in trial yet were not convicted.
    B. He picked them at random from the telephone book.
    C. At one time or another, all had vacationed at a certain hotel.
    D. All were guilty of murder, yet the law could not touch them.

20. How did the killer manage to complete the scheme without being caught by the others?
    A. He hid in the cave on the south side of the island.
    B. She seduced Philip Lombard into helping her.
    C. He managed to hide in a closet behind a fake wall in the dining room.
    D. Wargrave faked his death with the help of Dr. Armstrong.

III. Complete Answer
1. Provide a character sketch for three of the guests of Indian Island. Be sure to explain both negative and positive character traits as well as give a description of the crime that each is accused of committing.

2. Where is the climax of the story? Justify your answer with evidence from the text.

IV. Vocabulary

| | | | |
|---|---|---|---|
| ____ 1. | SURREPTITIOUS | A. | In a doubtful manner |
| ____ 2. | IMPROMPTU | B. | Strong feeling of dislike, opposition, or repugnance |
| ____ 3. | CONCURRED | C. | Private or secret meeting |
| ____ 4. | INERT | D. | Was of the same opinion; agreed |
| ____ 5. | STAMINA | E. | Made or done without previous preparation |
| ____ 6. | SERENELY | F. | Look or expression of the face |
| ____ 7. | FEASIBLE | G. | Capable of being done, effected, or accomplished |
| ____ 8. | OBLIVION | H. | State of being completely forgotten or unknown |
| ____ 9. | AVERSION | I. | Deliberately harmful or spiteful |
| ____ 10. | COUNTENANCE | J. | Unable to move or act |
| ____ 11. | MALICIOUS | K. | In a calm, peaceful, or tranquil manner |
| ____ 12. | AFFABLY | L. | Taking pains to avoid being observed; cautious; stealthy |
| ____ 13. | CONCLAVE | M. | False show of something |
| ____ 14. | PRETENCE | N. | Physical or moral strength to resist or withstand illness, fatigue, or hardship; endurance |
| ____ 15. | DUBIOUSLY | O. | In a friendly, cordial manner |

*And Then There Were None* Multiple Choice Unit Test 1 Answer Key

I. Matching

| | | | | |
|---|---|---|---|---|
| K | 1. | VERA | A. | Philip Lombard brought this weapon to the island. |
| E | 2. | MARSTON | B. | Vera's hired position with Mrs. Owen |
| G | 3. | EMILY | C. | Rogers was killed with this. |
| H | 4. | BLORE | D. | Emily noticed one on the dining room window. |
| V | 5. | TAYLOR | E. | Killed someone by being too reckless |
| R | 6. | CYRIL | F. | Marston's cause of death |
| S | 7. | DAVIS | G. | Led someone to suicide through moral judgment |
| Y | 8. | BRADY | H. | Committed perjury which led to the death of an innocent man |
| A | 9. | REVOLVER | I. | Author of *And Then There Were None* |
| W | 10. | INDIAN | J. | False clue in a murder mystery: a red ___ |
| T | 11. | BOAT | K. | Allowed a weak young boy to drown |
| B | 12. | SECRETARY | L. | Emily was missing it, and it turned up on the judge. |
| N | 13. | BUTLER | M. | Emily's pastime |
| P | 14. | BEACH | N. | Job of Mr. Rogers |
| U | 15. | CLOCK | O. | This curtain was missing from the bathroom. |
| C | 16. | AXE | P. | Where Armstrong's body was found |
| F | 17. | POISON | Q. | Vera's means of death |
| Q | 18. | HANGING | R. | Drowned when allowed to swim too far out to sea |
| L | 19. | YARN | S. | Mr. Blore's assumed name when he arrived on the island |
| J | 20. | HERRING | T. | The guests anxiously awaited its arrival, but it never came. |
| X | 21. | MURDER | U. | Blore was killed with this item. |
| M | 22. | KNITTING | V. | Beatrice's last name |
| O | 23. | OILSILK | W. | Ten of these figures were on the table in the beginning. |
| D | 24. | BEE | X. | The "voice" accused each of the guests of this. |
| I | 25. | CHRISTIE | Y. | Died after necessary medicine was withheld |

II. Multiple Choice

A 1.  Why is Vera Claythorne going to Indian Island?
   A. She is to serve as temporary secretary to Mrs. Owen.
   B. She is getting married on the island.
   C. She is meeting old friends for a holiday.
   D. She is the new cook for Mrs. Owen.

C 2.  What warning does Blore receive from the old man on the train?
   A. He'd better be properly dressed for the upcoming storm.
   B. The old man tells him to stay away from Indian Island.
   C. The old man tells him that the day of judgment is very close at hand.
   D. The old man tells Blore that someone is out to kill him.

B 3.  What hangs above the mantelpiece in each of the bedrooms in the island mansion?
   A. A seascape
   B. A framed nursery rhyme
   C. A map of the island
   D. A gruesome picture of Mr. U.N. Owen

D 4.  What reason does Emily Brent give for coming to Indian Island?
   A. One of her former students had recommended the Island as a wonderful vacation spot.
   B. Her doctor told her that a vacation by the sea would be good for her poor health.
   C. She is hired as the new cook on Indian Island.
   D. She said she is meeting an old friend who had invited her for a holiday.

C 5.  Of what crime does the "voice" accuse each person in the house?
   A. Arson
   B. Adultery
   C. Murder
   D. Extortion

A 6.  What accusation is made against Wargrave?
   A. He sentenced an innocent man to death.
   B. He killed his wife in a jealous rage.
   C. He killed his employer for a legacy left in her will.
   D. He ran over some children while speeding in his car.

140

C 7.   What discovery does Rogers make when he goes to clear the dinner dishes from the dining room?
   A. He finds all the dishes in the dining room smashed.
   B. He notices that someone has left the window open.
   C. He notices that one of the china figures is missing.
   D. He finds a small empty vial lying on the floor.

B 8.   What does Emily Brent suspect about Mr. and Mrs. Rogers?
   A. She suspects that they will attempt to leave the island, abandoning the group.
   B. She suspects that they killed their employer for the legacy.
   C. She suspects that they are slowly poisoning the guests with the meals.
   D. She suspects that they are in league with Mr. Owen to destroy them.

D 9.   Why doesn't Lombard believe that Mrs. Rogers killed herself?
   A. She was already nearly unconscious when she was put under a sedative.
   B. She did not have the courage to go through with something like that.
   C. She could not have injected herself with the syringe because she was hysterical.
   D. It is too soon after the death of Tony Marston to be a second suicide.

A 10.  After searching the entire house, what do Armstrong, Blore, and Lombard conclude?
   A. There is no one on the island but the occupants of the house.
   B. There is no murderer; the two deaths must have been suicides after all.
   C. The murderer must have left using the steps carved into the cliff.
   D. The murderer must be hiding in the cave on the south side of the island.

C 11.  Whose name does Emily Brent write in her diary as the murderer?
   A. Dr. Armstrong
   B. Philip Lombard
   C. Beatrice Taylor
   D. Vera Claythorne

D 12.  What does Blore confess to Lombard?
   A. He was hired to make sure no one leaves the island.
   B. He killed General Macarthur.
   C. He is Mr. Owen.
   D. He perjured himself and put an innocent man in prison where the man later died.

B 13.   Emily Brent dreams of Beatrice Taylor. What is Beatrice doing in the dream?
- A. Beatrice is killing Hugo.
- B. Beatrice is pressing her face against the window and moaning, asking to be let in.
- C. Beatrice is laughing at Emily.
- D. Beatrice is throwing her baby into the sea.

A 14.   Who immediately falls under suspicion for Emily's murder?
- A. Dr. Armstrong
- B. Vera
- C. Mr. Blore
- D. Judge Wargrave

D 15.   When Mr. Justice Wargrave is discovered dead what is strange about his appearance?
- A. He is dressed like a General.
- B. He appears to be sleeping.
- C. He is holding the missing revolver.
- D. He is dressed as a judge with a grey wig (the missing yarn) and a scarlet "robe" (the missing oilsilk).

C 16.   How does Lombard suggest the survivors make contact with people on the mainland?
- A. He thinks they could build a signal fire when the rain stops.
- B. He suggests using the telephone, but it is disconnected.
- C. He suggests using a mirror to heliograph an S O S.
- D. He suggests standing on the beach waving white clothing as flags.

C 17.   Vera believes someone is waiting for her in her bedroom. Who?
- A. Philip
- B. Cyril
- C. Hugo
- D. Isaac Morris

D 18.   Why had the people of Sticklehaven not attempted to make contact with anyone on Indian Island?
- A. The storm had made all communication impossible, even though they tried.
- B. They didn't know the owner, so they didn't bother.
- C. They hadn't noticed anything peculiar going on, so they didn't even think about the island.
- D. Mr. Morris told them that there was a contest on the island and to ignore all signals.

D 19.    Why did the murderer decide on these particular ten victims?
   A. They had all come before him in trial yet were not convicted.
   B. He picked them at random from the telephone book.
   C. At one time or another, all had vacationed at a certain hotel.
   D. All were guilty of murder, yet the law could not touch them.


D 20.    How did the killer manage to complete the scheme without being caught by the others?
   A. He hid in the cave on the south side of the island.
   B. She seduced Philip Lombard into helping her.
   C. He managed to hide in a closet behind a fake wall in the dining room.
   D. Wargrave faked his death with the help of Dr. Armstrong.

IV. Vocabulary

| | | | | |
|---|---|---|---|---|
| L | 1. | SURREPTITIOUS | A. | In a doubtful manner |
| E | 2. | IMPROMPTU | B. | Strong feeling of dislike, opposition, or repugnance |
| D | 3. | CONCURRED | C. | Private or secret meeting |
| J | 4. | INERT | D. | Was of the same opinion; agreed |
| N | 5. | STAMINA | E. | Made or done without previous preparation |
| K | 6. | SERENELY | F. | Look or expression of the face |
| G | 7. | FEASIBLE | G. | Capable of being done, effected, or accomplished |
| H | 8. | OBLIVION | H. | State of being completely forgotten or unknown |
| B | 9. | AVERSION | I. | Deliberately harmful or spiteful |
| F | 10. | COUNTENANCE | J. | Unable to move or act |
| I | 11. | MALICIOUS | K. | In a calm, peaceful, or tranquil manner |
| O | 12. | AFFABLY | L. | Taking pains to avoid being observed; cautious; stealthy |
| C | 13. | CONCLAVE | M. | False show of something |
| M | 14. | PRETENCE | N. | Physical or moral strength to resist or withstand illness, fatigue, or hardship; endurance |
| A | 15. | DUBIOUSLY | O. | In a friendly, cordial manner |

*And Then There Were None* Multiple Choice Unit Test 2

I. Matching

____ 1. ROGERS         A. Author of *And Then There Were None*
____ 2. VERA           B. Famous for making harsh judgments
____ 3. MARSTON        C. Led someone to suicide through moral judgment
____ 4. MACARTHUR      D. Captain of the boat that took the guests to Indian Island
____ 5. EMILY          E. Had an affair with his friend's wife
____ 6. PHILLIP        F. Mr. Blore's assumed name when he arrived on the island
____ 7. BLORE          G. Wargrave "cooked HIS goose."
____ 8. WARGRAVE       H. Knew that murder had been committed in order to win his love
____ 9. BEATRICE       I. Killed someone by being too reckless
____ 10. ARTHUR        J. Drowned when allowed to swim too far out to sea
____ 11. HUGO          K. Killed someone for sleeping with his wife
____ 12. CYRIL         L. Killed an employer by withholding medicine
____ 13. MORRIS        M. Committed perjury which led to the death of an innocent man
____ 14. NARRACOTT     N. Died after necessary medicine was withheld
____ 15. DAVIS         O. Conducted the purchase of Indian Island for an unnamed third party
____ 16. OWEN          P. Run down by a reckless driver
____ 17. COMBES        Q. Mr. Lombard's first name
____ 18. BRADY         R. The supposed owner of the island: Mr. U. N. ___
____ 19. SETON         S. Drowned herself after becoming pregnant
____ 20. CHRISTIE      T. Allowed a weak young boy to drown

II. Multiple Choice

1. What seems to be Dr. Armstrong's "specialty"?
    A. He performs illegal abortions.
    B. He is a plastic surgeon.
    C. He cons rich women with fake diagnoses to imagined illnesses.
    D. He assists terminally ill patients commit suicide.

2. What hangs above the mantelpiece in each of the bedrooms in the island mansion?
    A. A seascape
    B. A map of the island
    C. A gruesome picture of Mr. U.N. Owen
    D. A framed nursery rhyme

3. What reason does Emily Brent give for coming to Indian Island?
    A. She is hired as the new cook on Indian Island.
    B. One of her former students had recommended the Island as a wonderful vacation spot.
    C. Her doctor told her that a vacation by the sea would be good for her poor health.
    D. She said she is meeting an old friend who had invited her for a holiday.

4. Of what crime does the "voice" accuse each person in the house?
    A. Murder
    B. Arson
    C. Extortion
    D. Adultery

5. What conclusion does Wargrave come to about the owner of the house?
    A. Because of his initials "U. N." and last name "Owen," he must be "unknown" to them.
    B. He is a rich man pulling a publicity stunt.
    C. He will be arriving late to confront them face-to-face.
    D. The owner of the house is really Rogers using a phony name.

6. Who is the one person who refuses to speak about the charges made against him/her?
    A. Anthony Marston
    B. Emily Brent
    C. Mrs. Rogers
    D. Vera Claythorne

7. What do Lombard and Armstrong conclude about the nursery rhyme?
   A. It is a childish attempt to unnerve the guests.
   B. It is the theme to some crazy murder mystery party and no one is actually dead.
   C. There must be a murderer hiding on the island.
   D. It meant nothing; it is merely coincidence.

8. How has Emily Brent decided to pass the time?
   A. Cooking
   B. Walking on the shoreline, looking for a boat
   C. Knitting on the terrace
   D. Reading her Bible

9. After searching the entire house, what do Armstrong, Blore, and Lombard conclude?
   A. The murderer must be hiding in the cave on the south side of the island.
   B. There is no one on the island but the occupants of the house.
   C. The murderer must have left using the steps carved into the cliff.
   D. There is no murderer; the two deaths must have been suicides after all.

10. What does Lombard confess actually brought him to Indian Island?
    A. He is Mr. Owen's son.
    B. He came to assassinate them all.
    C. He was paid one hundred guineas to come and keep his eyes open.
    D. He knew that Vera Claythorne would be on the island, and he is in love with her.

11. Who immediately falls under suspicion for Emily's murder?
    A. Vera
    B. Judge Wargrave
    C. Mr. Blore
    D. Dr. Armstrong

12. What foods are the survivors reduced to eating?
    A. Macaroni and cheese
    B. Canned sardines
    C. Salted pork
    D. Tinned tongue

13. What does Vera suddenly remember about the nursery rhyme that makes the party think that Dr. Armstrong is still alive?
    A. A person is too large to be swallowed by a tiny fish, so Armstrong cannot be dead.
    B. Remembering how the fourth Indian boy died, it doesn't fit Armstrong's disappearance.
    C. She remembers the line about the red herring and believes they have been tricked.
    D. Armstrong never went to Chancery.

14. What do Vera and Lombard find that ends up pitting them against each other?
    A. They find a boat that is only big enough for one person.
    B. They find the larder is nearly out of food; there isn't enough for two people.
    C. They find the revolver lying on the beach.
    D. They find Armstrong's drowned body by the beach.

15. How does Vera Claythorne die?
    A. She takes poison.
    B. Philip Lombard shoots her.
    C. She hangs herself.
    D. She falls and breaks her neck.

16. What does the Assistant Commissioner of Scotland Yard find on Indian Island?
    A. The mansion has been burned down.
    B. He finds Philip Lombard barely alive, but breathing.
    C. There are ten dead bodies and not a living soul on the island.
    D. The island is completely deserted.

17. How do the police manage to solve the crime of Indian Island?
    A. Philip Lombard is still alive and he confessed.
    B. They find the confession on the dining room table next to the ten Indian boy figurines
    C. They hire Sherlock Holmes to solve the mystery.
    D. A fisherman finds a confession in a sealed bottle floating in the water.

18. Who was the murderer on Indian Island?
    A. Philip Lombard
    B. Vera Claythorne
    C. Judge Wargrave
    D. Emily Brent

19. Why did the murderer decide on these particular ten victims?
    A. At one time or another, all had vacationed at a certain hotel.
    B. He picked them at random from the telephone book.
    C. They had all come before him in trial yet were not convicted.
    D. All were guilty of murder, yet the law could not touch them.

III. Complete Answer
1. Describe the setting of the novel. What particular elements of the setting help create an atmosphere of mystery and suspense?

2. How does the author's use of the nursery rhyme throughout the novel add to the creation of suspense?

3. Choose any two characters and compare and contrast the way they reacted to and dealt with the situation.

4. Did all of the "guests" deserve to die? If so, explain why. If not, who did not? Why not?

IV. Vocabulary

____ 1. SUBSEQUENT         A. Of the highest kind, quality, or order; surpassing all else or others

____ 2. DEPORTMENT         B. Undertaking involving uncertainty as to the outcome

____ 3. VENTURE            C. Characterized by a hypocritical concern with virtue or religious devotion

____ 4. SUPERLATIVELY      D. Indefinitely long period of time

____ 5. INDICTMENTS        E. Made or done without previous preparation

____ 6. UNOBTRUSIVELY      F. Expertise or nimbleness in the use of the hands or body

____ 7. IMPROMPTU          G. Deliberately harmful or spiteful

____ 8. CONCURRED          H. Private or secret meeting

____ 9. RECONNAISSANCE     I. In a manner that is not undesirably noticeable or blatant

____ 10. COVERTLY          J. Capable of being done, effected, or accomplished

____ 11. INERT             K. Occurring or coming later or after

____ 12. PIOUS             L. Search made for useful military information in the field

____ 13. FEASIBLE          M. Secretly; in a concealed manner

____ 14. STILETTO          N. Act of accusing in return

____ 15. COUNTENANCE       O. Written statements charging a party with the commission of a crime

____ 16. MALICIOUS         P. Unable to move or act

____ 17. RECRIMINATION     Q. Demeanor; conduct; behavior

____ 18. CONCLAVE          R. A small dagger with a slender, tapering blade

____ 19. AEONS             S. Look or expression of the face

____ 20. INCLINATION       T. Disposition or bent, esp. of the mind or will; a liking or preference

____ 21. ADROITNESS        U. Was of the same opinion; agreed

*And Then There Were None* Multiple Choice Unit Test 2 Answer Key

I. Matching

| | | | | |
|---|---|---|---|---|
| L | 1. | ROGERS | A. | Author of *And Then There Were None* |
| T | 2. | VERA | B. | Famous for making harsh judgments |
| I | 3. | MARSTON | C. | Led someone to suicide through moral judgment |
| K | 4. | MACARTHUR | D. | Captain of the boat that took the guests to Indian Island |
| C | 5. | EMILY | E. | Had an affair with his friend's wife |
| Q | 6. | PHILLIP | F. | Mr. Blore's assumed name when he arrived on the island |
| M | 7. | BLORE | G. | Wargrave "cooked HIS goose." |
| B | 8. | WARGRAVE | H. | Knew that murder had been committed in order to win his love |
| S | 9. | BEATRICE | I. | Killed someone by being too reckless |
| E | 10. | ARTHUR | J. | Drowned when allowed to swim too far out to sea |
| H | 11. | HUGO | K. | Killed someone for sleeping with his wife |
| J | 12. | CYRIL | L. | Killed an employer by withholding medicine |
| O | 13. | MORRIS | M. | Committed perjury which led to the death of an innocent man |
| D | 14. | NARRACOTT | N. | Died after necessary medicine was withheld |
| F | 15. | DAVIS | O. | Conducted the purchase of Indian Island for an unnamed third party |
| R | 16. | OWEN | P. | Run down by a reckless driver |
| P | 17. | COMBES | Q. | Mr. Lombard's first name |
| N | 18. | BRADY | R. | The supposed owner of the island: Mr. U. N. ___ |
| G | 19. | SETON | S. | Drowned herself after becoming pregnant |
| A | 20. | CHRISTIE | T. | Allowed a weak young boy to drown |

II. Multiple Choice

C 1. What seems to be Dr. Armstrong's "specialty"?
   A. He performs illegal abortions.
   B. He is a plastic surgeon.
   C. He cons rich women with fake diagnoses to imagined illnesses.
   D. He assists terminally ill patients commit suicide.

D 2. What hangs above the mantelpiece in each of the bedrooms in the island mansion?
   A. A seascape
   B. A map of the island
   C. A gruesome picture of Mr. U.N. Owen
   D. A framed nursery rhyme

D 3. What reason does Emily Brent give for coming to Indian Island?
   A. She is hired as the new cook on Indian Island.
   B. One of her former students had recommended the Island as a wonderful vacation spot.
   C. Her doctor told her that a vacation by the sea would be good for her poor health.
   D. She said she is meeting an old friend who had invited her for a holiday.

A 4. Of what crime does the "voice" accuse each person in the house?
   A. Murder
   B. Arson
   C. Extortion
   D. Adultery

A 5. What conclusion does Wargrave come to about the owner of the house?
   A. Because of his initials "U. N." and last name "Owen," he must be "unknown" to them.
   B. He is a rich man pulling a publicity stunt.
   C. He will be arriving late to confront them face-to-face.
   D. The owner of the house is really Rogers using a phony name.

B 6. Who is the one person who refuses to speak about the charges made against him/her?
   A. Anthony Marston
   B. Emily Brent
   C. Mrs. Rogers
   D. Vera Claythorne

C 7.  What do Lombard and Armstrong conclude about the nursery rhyme?
  A. It is a childish attempt to unnerve the guests.
  B. It is the theme to some crazy murder mystery party and no one is actually dead.
  C. There must be a murderer hiding on the island.
  D. It meant nothing; it is merely coincidence.

C 8.  How has Emily Brent decided to pass the time?
  A. Cooking
  B. Walking on the shoreline, looking for a boat
  C. Knitting on the terrace
  D. Reading her Bible

B 9.  After searching the entire house, what do Armstrong, Blore, and Lombard conclude?
  A. The murderer must be hiding in the cave on the south side of the island.
  B. There is no one on the island but the occupants of the house.
  C. The murderer must have left using the steps carved into the cliff.
  D. There is no murderer; the two deaths must have been suicides after all.

C 10.  What does Lombard confess actually brought him to Indian Island?
  A. He is Mr. Owen's son.
  B. He came to assassinate them all.
  C. He was paid one hundred guineas to come and keep his eyes open.
  D. He knew that Vera Claythorne would be on the island, and he is in love with her.

D 11.  Who immediately falls under suspicion for Emily's murder?
  A. Vera
  B. Judge Wargrave
  C. Mr. Blore
  D. Dr. Armstrong

D 12.  What foods are the survivors reduced to eating?
  A. Macaroni and cheese
  B. Canned sardines
  C. Salted pork
  D. Tinned tongue

155

C 13.  What does Vera suddenly remember about the nursery rhyme that makes the party think that Dr. Armstrong is still alive?
   A. A person is too large to be swallowed by a tiny fish, so Armstrong cannot be dead.
   B. Remembering how the fourth Indian boy died, it doesn't fit Armstrong's disappearance.
   C. She remembers the line about the red herring and believes they have been tricked.
   D. Armstrong never went to Chancery.

D 14.  What do Vera and Lombard find that ends up pitting them against each other?
   A. They find a boat that is only big enough for one person.
   B. They find the larder is nearly out of food; there isn't enough for two people.
   C. They find the revolver lying on the beach.
   D. They find Armstrong's drowned body by the beach.

C 15.  How does Vera Claythorne die?
   A. She takes poison.
   B. Philip Lombard shoots her.
   C. She hangs herself.
   D. She falls and breaks her neck.

C 16.  What does the Assistant Commissioner of Scotland Yard find on Indian Island?
   A. The mansion has been burned down.
   B. He finds Philip Lombard barely alive, but breathing.
   C. There are ten dead bodies and not a living soul on the island.
   D. The island is completely deserted.

D 17.  How do the police manage to solve the crime of Indian Island?
   A. Philip Lombard is still alive and he confessed.
   B. They find the confession on the dining room table next to the ten Indian boy figurines
   C. They hire Sherlock Holmes to solve the mystery.
   D. A fisherman finds a confession in a sealed bottle floating in the water.

C 18.  Who was the murderer on Indian Island?
   A. Philip Lombard
   B. Vera Claythorne
   C. Judge Wargrave
   D. Emily Brent

D 19. Why did the murderer decide on these particular ten victims?
	A. At one time or another, all had vacationed at a certain hotel.
	B. He picked them at random from the telephone book.
	C. They had all come before him in trial yet were not convicted.
	D. All were guilty of murder, yet the law could not touch them.

IV. Vocabulary

| | | | |
|---|---|---|---|
| K | 1. SUBSEQUENT | A. | Of the highest kind, quality, or order; surpassing all else or others |
| Q | 2. DEPORTMENT | B. | Undertaking involving uncertainty as to the outcome |
| B | 3. VENTURE | C. | Characterized by a hypocritical concern with virtue or religious devotion |
| A | 4. SUPERLATIVELY | D. | Indefinitely long period of time |
| O | 5. INDICTMENTS | E. | Made or done without previous preparation |
| I | 6. UNOBTRUSIVELY | F. | Expertise or nimbleness in the use of the hands or body |
| E | 7. IMPROMPTU | G. | Deliberately harmful or spiteful |
| U | 8. CONCURRED | H. | Private or secret meeting |
| L | 9. RECONNAISSANCE | I. | In a manner that is not undesirably noticeable or blatant |
| M | 10. COVERTLY | J. | Capable of being done, effected, or accomplished |
| P | 11. INERT | K. | Occurring or coming later or after |
| C | 12. PIOUS | L. | Search made for useful military information in the field |
| J | 13. FEASIBLE | M. | Secretly; in a concealed manner |
| R | 14. STILETTO | N. | Act of accusing in return |
| S | 15. COUNTENANCE | O. | Written statements charging a party with the commission of a crime |
| G | 16. MALICIOUS | P. | Unable to move or act |
| N | 17. RECRIMINATION | Q. | Demeanor; conduct; behavior |
| H | 18. CONCLAVE | R. | A small dagger with a slender, tapering blade |
| D | 19. AEONS | S. | Look or expression of the face |
| T | 20. INCLINATION | T. | Disposition or bent, esp. of the mind or will; a liking or preference |
| F | 21. ADROITNESS | U. | Was of the same opinion; agreed |

# UNIT RESOURCE MATERIALS

# BULLETIN BOARD IDEAS *And Then There Were None*

1. Save one corner of the board for the best of students' *And Then There Were None* writing assignments.
2. Take one of the word search puzzles from the extra activities packet and with a marker copy it over in a large size on the bulletin board. Write the clue words to find to one side. Invite students prior to and after class to find the words and circle them on the bulletin board.
3. Write several of the most significant quotations from the book onto the board on brightly colored paper.
4. Make a bulletin board listing the vocabulary words for this unit. As you complete sections of the novel and discuss the vocabulary for each section, write the definitions on the bulletin board. (If your board is one students face frequently, it will help them learn the words.)
5. Make a bulletin board dedicated to the history of the murder mystery genre.
6. Make a bulletin board dedicated to Dame Agatha Christie and her works. She has such a volume of works! Have each of your students read a summary of a different book by Agatha Christie, and have each student make a book jacket for the story he/she read. Post the book jackets on the board.
7. Make a bulletin board dedicated to Agatha Christie's most famous detectives Hercule Poirot and Miss Marple.
8. Create a bulletin board for the nursery rhyme, being sure to illustrate it with pictures of each character as they relate to the Indian boys.
9. Create a store display to market your class board games.
10. Make a newspaper bulletin board with articles students write about the mysterious murders on Indian Island.
11. Make an "unsolved mysteries" bulletin board.
12. Create a bulletin board dedicated to one or more of the topics from Writing Assignment #2.

## RELATED TOPICS *And Then There Were None*

1. Unsolved Mysteries
2. Firearm Safety
3. Knitting
4. The Worst Generals In History
5. Medical Malpractice
6. Vigilante Justice
7. Criminals On Death Row
8. Careers in Detective/Police Work, Law, Medicine, Secretarial Work, etc.
9. Riddles
10. Other Books By Agatha Christie
11. Deductive Reasoning
12. Investigative Techniques
13. The British Judicial System
14. Stories by Edgar Allan Poe, Sir Arthur Conan Doyle, Ellery Queen, etc.
15. British Society In The Early 20th Century
16. Private Islands

## MORE ACTIVITIES *And Then There Were None*

1. Agatha Christie used the children's nursery rhyme *Ten Little Indians* as the basis for her plot. Select another nursery rhyme and create a plot line for a story related to the rhyme.
2. Hosting a Murder Mystery Party in the classroom is fun. There are many games that can be downloaded from the Internet for a modest fee, but once you have them, they can be used again and again. Suggested sites:

   *Murder Mystery Games for Kids and Teens*
   http://www.dinnerandamurder.com/games/kids.htm

   *Clean and Teen Murder Mysteries*
   http://www.nightofmystery.com/Clean_Murder_mysteries.php

   *Murder Mystery Maniacs: Teen Murder Mysteries*
   http://www.host-a-murder.com/teen.html

3. Create a debate about the appropriateness of teaching murder mysteries in public schools. For those who resist the novel based on the murder plot line, this is their time to defend their position. Be sure to follow proper debate procedures. Some informational sites are:

   *Teacher Vision: Lincoln-Douglas Style Debate* (most common format used by Speech and Debate/Forensics teams)
   http://www.teachervision.fen.com/us-civil-war/lesson-plan/2543.html

   *Debate Procedure*
   http://courses.cs.vt.edu/~cs3604/support/Assignments/Final.Assmt.S99/Section2/Grp4/debateprocedures.html

4. Create a spoof or parody of *And Then There Were None*. Films like *Scary Movie* (1-4) and *Shawn of the Dead* parodied famous horror films. Each character from *And Then There Were None* could be an individual parody of an element of society or the entire work could parody murder mystery television shows (*Murder, She Wrote*, *Columbo*, or *Diagnosis, Murder*).
5. Have students design a book cover (front and back and inside flaps) for *And Then There Were None*.
6. Have students design a bulletin board (ready to be put up; not just sketched) for *And Then There Were None*.
7. Have students write out the characters in the book and cast famous actors and actress for a movie version of the novel. Instruct students to write a brief explanation as to why the actor/actress they selected would be perfect for the part.

## UNIT WORD LIST *And Then There Were None*

| No. | Word | Clue/Definition |
|---|---|---|
| 1. | ARTHUR | Had an affair with his friend's wife |
| 2. | AXE | Rogers was killed with this. |
| 3. | BEACH | Where Armstrong's body was found |
| 4. | BEAR | The marble clock was in this shape. |
| 5. | BEATRICE | Drowned herself after becoming pregnant |
| 6. | BEE | Emily noticed one on the dining room window. |
| 7. | BLORE | Committed perjury which led to the death of an innocent man |
| 8. | BLUDGEONING | General Macarthur's cause of death |
| 9. | BOAT | The guests anxiously awaited its arrival, but it never came. |
| 10. | BOTTLE | A fisherman found the confession in this. |
| 11. | BRADY | Died after necessary medicine was withheld |
| 12. | BRENT | Emily's last name |
| 13. | BUTLER | Job of Mr. Rogers |
| 14. | CHRISTIE | Author of *And Then There Were None* |
| 15. | CLAYTHORNE | Vera's last name |
| 16. | CLEES | Died on the operating table |
| 17. | CLOCK | Blore was killed with this item. |
| 18. | COMBES | Run down by a reckless driver |
| 19. | CYRIL | Drowned when allowed to swim too far out to sea |
| 20. | DAVIS | Mr. Blore's assumed name when he arrived on the island |
| 21. | EMILY | Led someone to suicide through moral judgment |
| 22. | ENGLAND | Country in which the story takes place |
| 23. | HANGING | Vera's means of death |
| 24. | HERRING | False clue in a murder mystery: a red ___ |
| 25. | HOOK | Vera noticed this in the ceiling near her bed. |
| 26. | HUGO | Knew that murder had been committed in order to win his love |
| 27. | INDIAN | Ten of these figures were on the table in the beginning. |
| 28. | ISLAND | Setting of the novel: Indian ___ |
| 29. | JUDGE | Wargrave's occupation |
| 30. | KNITTING | Emily's pastime |
| 31. | LITTLE | Original title: Ten ___ Indians |
| 32. | LOMBARD | Abandoned a group of men under attack |
| 33. | MACARTHUR | Killed someone for sleeping with his wife |
| 34. | MARSTON | Killed someone by being too reckless |
| 35. | MORRIS | Conducted the purchase of Indian Island for an unnamed third party |
| 36. | MURDER | The "voice" accused each of the guests of this. |
| 37. | NARRACOTT | Captain of the boat that took the guests to Indian Island |
| 38. | NURSERY | The murders followed the ___ rhyme. |

| No. | Word | Clue/Definition |
|---|---|---|
| 39. | OILSILK | This curtain was missing from the bathroom. |
| 40. | OWEN | The supposed owner of the island: Mr. U. N. ___ |
| 41. | PHILLIP | Mr. Lombard's first name |
| 42. | POE | Credited as inventor of the murder mystery genre |
| 43. | POISON | Marston's cause of death |
| 44. | REVOLVER | Philip Lombard brought this weapon to the island. |
| 45. | ROGERS | Killed an employer by withholding medicine |
| 46. | SECRETARY | Vera's hired position with Mrs. Owen |
| 47. | SETON | Wargrave "cooked HIS goose." |
| 48. | SWAN | Title of the song on the gramophone: ___ Song |
| 49. | SYRINGE | Armstrong was missing this item from his bag. |
| 50. | TAYLOR | Beatrice's last name |
| 51. | TONGUE | The group was reduced to eating this. |
| 52. | TORTOISE | Wargrave was said to look like a "wary old ___." |
| 53. | VERA | Allowed a weak young boy to drown |
| 54. | WARGRAVE | Famous for making harsh judgments |
| 55. | YARN | Emily was missing it, and it turned up on the judge. |

# And Then There Were None Word Search

```
R E V O L V E R O Z C N B D W B K I B M Z D C Z
G G F D V Y M X I Z O M N C H L P N N O C C Y F
N X K L J L P T L T T S F A Q O F C I D T B R H
L H Y B B V F O S Z A X G R X R H T L T I T I X
C O M B E S C R I W Y J U D G E H O O K T A L Q
S T M O A A A T L S L N S M R F B G M N D I N E
N T P B T M R O K N O G E R B T U E B N G Q N P
B O A T R Y L I M E R N I N L H E Y A R N U R G
K C Q G I A Y S Y W R N A O U B S L R C E U E S
K A Z J C R D E M O G W Q T D R S Y D K H N X M
B R L J E E J Y H R S B S E G I S M R T X S T B
Y R S T X V L T E J M R E S E G Q E R I I M N N
Q A C V R Z Y L H M E G E H O N R A R R N S W X
D N J D M A T N W G A S L N N I N Z R Y H G Z Y
Z D T V L U B J O A D C C P I G E O P P Y H E R
K A X C B N R R H F R T A X N N M X H C E Y M L
D V X W B D S D V Z T G K R G A C H I M L R F K
M I T J Q S L L E J M H R L T H D H L M T O M R
N S S E C R E T A R Y W A A X H P Y L K T G C Q
B V F S B C D G G Y W N V J V X U Z I K I P P K
C H R I S T I E D Y D D X B K E L R P C L X H R
```

| | | | |
|---|---|---|---|
| ARTHUR | CLAYTHORNE | JUDGE | POISON |
| AXE | CLEES | KNITTING | REVOLVER |
| BEACH | CLOCK | LITTLE | ROGERS |
| BEAR | COMBES | LOMBARD | SECRETARY |
| BEATRICE | CYRIL | MACARTHUR | SETON |
| BEE | DAVIS | MARSTON | SWAN |
| BLORE | EMILY | MORRIS | SYRINGE |
| BLUDGEONING | ENGLAND | MURDER | TAYLOR |
| BOAT | HANGING | NARRACOTT | TONGUE |
| BOTTLE | HERRING | NURSERY | TORTOISE |
| BRADY | HOOK | OILSILK | VERA |
| BRENT | HUGO | OWEN | WARGRAVE |
| BUTLER | INDIAN | PHILLIP | YARN |
| CHRISTIE | ISLAND | POE | |

# And Then There Were None Word Search Answer Key

| ARTHUR | CLAYTHORNE | JUDGE | POISON |
| AXE | CLEES | KNITTING | REVOLVER |
| BEACH | CLOCK | LITTLE | ROGERS |
| BEAR | COMBES | LOMBARD | SECRETARY |
| BEATRICE | CYRIL | MACARTHUR | SETON |
| BEE | DAVIS | MARSTON | SWAN |
| BLORE | EMILY | MORRIS | SYRINGE |
| BLUDGEONING | ENGLAND | MURDER | TAYLOR |
| BOAT | HANGING | NARRACOTT | TONGUE |
| BOTTLE | HERRING | NURSERY | TORTOISE |
| BRADY | HOOK | OILSILK | VERA |
| BRENT | HUGO | OWEN | WARGRAVE |
| BUTLER | INDIAN | PHILLIP | YARN |
| CHRISTIE | ISLAND | POE | |

# And Then There Were None Crossword

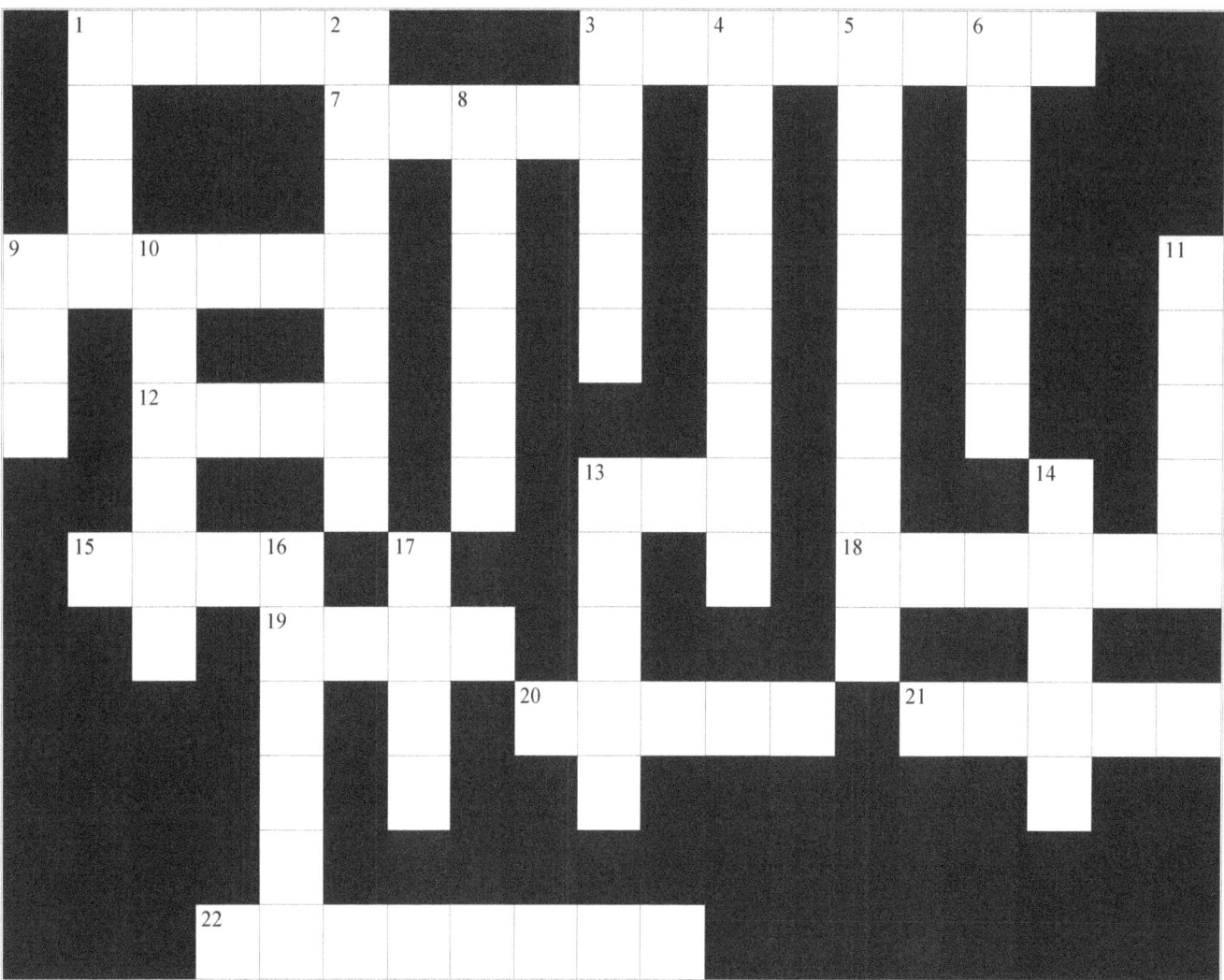

Across
1. Where Armstrong's body was found
3. Author of And Then There Were None
7. Led someone to suicide through moral judgment
9. Had an affair with his friend's wife
12. Emily was missing it, and it turned up on the judge.
13. Emily noticed one on the dining room window.
15. The guests anxiously awaited its arrival, but it never came.
18. Killed an employer by withholding medicine
19. Supposed owner of the island: Mr. U. N. ___
20. Died after necessary medicine was withheld
21. Blore was killed with this item.
22. Drowned herself after becoming pregnant.

Down
1. The marble clock was in this shape
2. False clue in a murder mystery: a red ___
3. Drowned when allowed to swim too far out to sea
4. Lombard brought this weapon to the island.
5. Vera's hired position with Mrs. Owen
6. Setting of the novel: Indian ___
8. Ten of these figures were on the table in the beginning.
9. Rogers was killed with this.
10. Beatrice's last name
11. Died on the operating table
13. Committed perjury which led to the death of an innocent man
14. Wargrave cooked HIS goose.
16. The group was reduced to eating this.
17. Allowed a weak young boy to drown

# And Then There Were None Crossword Answer Key

Across
1. Where Armstrong's body was found
3. Author of And Then There Were None
7. Led someone to suicide through moral judgment
9. Had an affair with his friend's wife
12. Emily was missing it, and it turned up on the judge.
13. Emily noticed one on the dining room window.
15. The guests anxiously awaited its arrival, but it never came.
18. Killed an employer by withholding medicine
19. Supposed owner of the island: Mr. U. N. ___
20. Died after necessary medicine was withheld
21. Blore was killed with this item.
22. Drowned herself after becoming pregnant.

Down
1. The marble clock was in this shape
2. False clue in a murder mystery: a red ___
3. Drowned when allowed to swim too far out to sea
4. Lombard brought this weapon to the island.
5. Vera's hired position with Mrs. Owen
6. Setting of the novel: Indian ___
8. Ten of these figures were on the table in the beginning.
9. Rogers was killed with this.
10. Beatrice's last name
11. Died on the operating table
13. Committed perjury which led to the death of an innocent man
14. Wargrave cooked HIS goose.
16. The group was reduced to eating this.
17. Allowed a weak young boy to drown

And Then There Were None Matching 1

___ 1. BUTLER           A. Where Armstrong's body was found
___ 2. SECRETARY        B. Setting of the novel: Indian ___
___ 3. BLUDGEONING      C. Credited as inventor of murder mystery genre
___ 4. POE              D. Country in which the story takes place
___ 5. YARN             E. Killed an employer by withholding medicine
___ 6. MACARTHUR        F. Emily was missing it, and it turned up on the judge.
___ 7. ISLAND           G. Original title: Ten ___ Indians
___ 8. OILSILK          H. Was run down by a reckless driver
___ 9. VERA             I. Drowned herself after becoming pregnant
___ 10. INDIAN          J. General Macarthur's cause of death
___ 11. BEACH           K. Supposed owner of the island: Mr. U. N. ___
___ 12. HOOK            L. Allowed a weak young boy to drown
___ 13. OWEN            M. Ten of these figures were on the table in the beginning.
___ 14. BEATRICE        N. Killed someone for sleeping with his wife
___ 15. WARGRAVE        O. Conducted the purchase of Indian Island for an unnamed third party
___ 16. MORRIS          P. Vera's hired position with Mrs. Owen
___ 17. LITTLE          Q. Famous for making harsh judgments
___ 18. HANGING         R. Marston's cause of death
___ 19. COMBES          S. The guests anxiously awaited its arrival, but it never came.
___ 20. POISON          T. Vera's means of death
___ 21. BOAT            U. Vera noticed this in the ceiling near her bed.
___ 22. ENGLAND         V. The group was reduced to eating this.
___ 23. ROGERS          W. This curtain was missing from the bathroom.
___ 24. CLEES           X. Job of Mr. Rogers
___ 25. TONGUE          Y. Died on the operating table

## And Then There Were None Matching 1 Answer Key

X - 1. BUTLER
P - 2. SECRETARY
J - 3. BLUDGEONING
C - 4. POE
F - 5. YARN
N - 6. MACARTHUR
B - 7. ISLAND
W  8. OILSILK
L - 9. VERA
M -10. INDIAN
A -11. BEACH
U -12. HOOK
K -13. OWEN
I - 14. BEATRICE
Q -15. WARGRAVE
O -16. MORRIS
G -17. LITTLE
T -18. HANGING
H -19. COMBES
R -20. POISON
S -21. BOAT
D -22. ENGLAND
E -23. ROGERS
Y -24. CLEES
V -25. TONGUE

A. Where Armstrong's body was found
B. Setting of the novel: Indian ___
C. Credited as inventor of murder mystery genre
D. Country in which the story takes place
E. Killed an employer by withholding medicine
F. Emily was missing it, and it turned up on the judge.
G. Original title: Ten ___ Indians
H. Was run down by a reckless driver
I. Drowned herself after becoming pregnant
J. General Macarthur's cause of death
K. Supposed owner of the island: Mr. U. N. ___
L. Allowed a weak young boy to drown
M. Ten of these figures were on the table in the beginning.
N. Killed someone for sleeping with his wife
O. Conducted the purchase of Indian Island for an unnamed third party
P. Vera's hired position with Mrs. Owen
Q. Famous for making harsh judgments
R. Marston's cause of death
S. The guests anxiously awaited its arrival, but it never came.
T. Vera's means of death
U. Vera noticed this in the ceiling near her bed.
V. The group was reduced to eating this.
W. This curtain was missing from the bathroom.
X. Job of Mr. Rogers
Y. Died on the operating table

And Then There Were None Matching 2

___ 1. MURDER         A. Emily's last name
___ 2. TAYLOR         B. Vera's hired position with Mrs. Owen
___ 3. BRENT          C. Famous for making harsh judgments
___ 4. BOAT           D. Wargrave's occupation
___ 5. COMBES         E. Setting of the novel: Indian ___
___ 6. JUDGE          F. The guests anxiously awaited its arrival, but it never came.
___ 7. CLAYTHORNE     G. Original title: Ten ___ Indians
___ 8. WARGRAVE       H. Lombard brought this weapon to the island.
___ 9. REVOLVER       I. Committed perjury which led to the death of an innocent man
___10. CYRIL          J. Wargrave cooked HIS goose.
___11. SECRETARY      K. This curtain was missing from the bathroom.
___12. OILSILK        L. Allowed a weak young boy to drown
___13. CLEES          M. Where Armstrong's body was found
___14. SETON          N. The voice accused each of the guests of this.
___15. AXE            O. Died on the operating table
___16. BEE            P. Conducted the purchase of Indian Island for an unnamed third party
___17. BRADY          Q. Was run down by a reckless driver
___18. LITTLE         R. Rogers was killed with this.
___19. BLORE          S. Drowned when allowed to swim too far out to sea
___20. DAVIS          T. Died after necessary medicine was withheld
___21. BEACH          U. Mr. Blore's assumed name when he arrived on the island
___22. BEAR           V. The marble clock was in this shape
___23. MORRIS         W. Vera's last name
___24. ISLAND         X. Beatrice's last name
___25. VERA           Y. Emily noticed one on the dining room window.

## And Then There Were None Matching 2 Answer Key

| | | |
|---|---|---|
| N - 1. MURDER | | A. Emily's last name |
| X - 2. TAYLOR | | B. Vera's hired position with Mrs. Owen |
| A - 3. BRENT | | C. Famous for making harsh judgments |
| F - 4. BOAT | | D. Wargrave's occupation |
| Q - 5. COMBES | | E. Setting of the novel: Indian ___ |
| D - 6. JUDGE | | F. The guests anxiously awaited its arrival, but it never came. |
| W - 7. CLAYTHORNE | | G. Original title: Ten ___ Indians |
| C - 8. WARGRAVE | | H. Lombard brought this weapon to the island. |
| H - 9. REVOLVER | | I. Committed perjury which led to the death of an innocent man |
| S - 10. CYRIL | | J. Wargrave cooked HIS goose. |
| B - 11. SECRETARY | | K. This curtain was missing from the bathroom. |
| K - 12. OILSILK | | L. Allowed a weak young boy to drown |
| O - 13. CLEES | | M. Where Armstrong's body was found |
| J - 14. SETON | | N. The voice accused each of the guests of this. |
| R - 15. AXE | | O. Died on the operating table |
| Y - 16. BEE | | P. Conducted the purchase of Indian Island for an unnamed third party |
| T - 17. BRADY | | Q. Was run down by a reckless driver |
| G - 18. LITTLE | | R. Rogers was killed with this. |
| I - 19. BLORE | | S. Drowned when allowed to swim too far out to sea |
| U - 20. DAVIS | | T. Died after necessary medicine was withheld |
| M - 21. BEACH | | U. Mr. Blore's assumed name when he arrived on the island |
| V - 22. BEAR | | V. The marble clock was in this shape |
| P - 23. MORRIS | | W. Vera's last name |
| E - 24. ISLAND | | X. Beatrice's last name |
| L - 25. VERA | | Y. Emily noticed one on the dining room window. |

And Then There Were None Juggle Letters 1

1. YCRNOETHAL = 1. _____
   Vera's last name

2. RBEA = 2. _____
   The marble clock was in this shape

3. TOAB = 3. _____
   The guests anxiously awaited its arrival, but it never came.

4. AMSTRNO = 4. _____
   Killed someone by being too reckless

5. YRAN = 5. _____
   Emily was missing it, and it turned up on the judge.

6. TEITLL = 6. _____
   Original title: Ten \_\_\_ Indians

7. OLDBRAM = 7. _____
   Abandoned a group of men under attack

8. ERNTB = 8. _____
   Emily's last name

9. UHRTRA = 9. _____
   Had an affair with his friend's wife

10. OKHO =10. _____
    Vera noticed this in the ceiling near her bed.

11. OUHG =11. _____
    Knew that murder had been committed to win his love

12. HECBA =12. _____
    Where Armstrong's body was found

13. LBERUT =13. _____
    Job of Mr. Rogers

14. OVELREVR =14. _____
    Lombard brought this weapon to the island.

15. NASW =15. _____
    Title of the song on the gramophone: \_\_\_ Song

## And Then There Were None Juggle Letters 1 Answer

1. YCRNOETHAL = 1. CLAYTHORNE
   Vera's last name

2. RBEA = 2. BEAR
   The marble clock was in this shape

3. TOAB = 3. BOAT
   The guests anxiously awaited its arrival, but it never came.

4. AMSTRNO = 4. MARSTON
   Killed someone by being too reckless

5. YRAN = 5. YARN
   Emily was missing it, and it turned up on the judge.

6. TEITLL = 6. LITTLE
   Original title: Ten ___ Indians

7. OLDBRAM = 7. LOMBARD
   Abandoned a group of men under attack

8. ERNTB = 8. BRENT
   Emily's last name

9. UHRTRA = 9. ARTHUR
   Had an affair with his friend's wife

10. OKHO = 10. HOOK
    Vera noticed this in the ceiling near her bed.

11. OUHG = 11. HUGO
    Knew that murder had been committed to win his love

12. HECBA = 12. BEACH
    Where Armstrong's body was found

13. LBERUT = 13. BUTLER
    Job of Mr. Rogers

14. OVELREVR = 14. REVOLVER
    Lombard brought this weapon to the island.

15. NASW = 15. SWAN
    Title of the song on the gramophone: ___ Song

## And Then There Were None Juggle Letters 2

1. RATTRNACO  = 1. _____
   Captain of the boat that took the guests to the island

2. RUTHRA  = 2. _____
   Had an affair with his friend's wife

3. EBOMSC  = 3. _____
   Was run down by a reckless driver

4. RLCYI  = 4. _____
   Drowned when allowed to swim too far out to sea

5. BLADROM  = 5. _____
   Abandoned a group of men under attack

6. INOSPO  = 6. _____
   Marston's cause of death

7. GOHU  = 7. _____
   Knew that murder had been committed to win his love

8. OSGRRE  = 8. _____
   Killed an employer by withholding medicine

9. NSEYIGR  = 9. _____
   Armstrong was missing this item from his bag.

10. YABDR  =10. _____
    Died after necessary medicine was withheld

11. SIIKLOL  =11. _____
    This curtain was missing from the bathroom.

12. VWREARAG  =12. _____
    Famous for making harsh judgments

13. RSAMONT  =13. _____
    Killed someone by being too reckless

14. ESTIROOT  =14. _____
    Wargrave was said to look like a wary old one of these.

15. RSIRMO  =15. _____
    Conducted the purchase of Indian Island for an unnamed third party

And Then There Were None Juggle Letters 2 Answer Key

1. RATTRNACO = 1. NARRACOTT
Captain of the boat that took the guests to the island

2. RUTHRA = 2. ARTHUR
Had an affair with his friend's wife

3. EBOMSC = 3. COMBES
Was run down by a reckless driver

4. RLCYI = 4. CYRIL
Drowned when allowed to swim too far out to sea

5. BLADROM = 5. LOMBARD
Abandoned a group of men under attack

6. INOSPO = 6. POISON
Marston's cause of death

7. GOHU = 7. HUGO
Knew that murder had been committed to win his love

8. OSGRRE = 8. ROGERS
Killed an employer by withholding medicine

9. NSEYIGR = 9. SYRINGE
Armstrong was missing this item from his bag.

10. YABDR =10. BRADY
Died after necessary medicine was withheld

11. SIIKLOL =11. OILSILK
This curtain was missing from the bathroom.

12. VWREARAG =12. WARGRAVE
Famous for making harsh judgments

13. RSAMONT =13. MARSTON
Killed someone by being too reckless

14. ESTIROOT =14. TORTOISE
Wargrave was said to look like a wary old one of these.

15. RSIRMO =15. MORRIS
Conducted the purchase of Indian Island for an unnamed third party

# VOCABULARY RESOURCE MATERIALS

# And Then There Were None Vocabulary Word List

| No. | Word | Clue/Definition |
|---|---|---|
| 1. | ABHORRENT | Detestable; loathsome; hateful |
| 2. | ABSTRACT | Theoretical; not applied or practical |
| 3. | ADMONITORY | Serving to warn, especially to correct |
| 4. | ADROITNESS | Expertise or nimbleness in the use of the hands or body |
| 5. | AEONS | Indefinitely long periods of time |
| 6. | AFFABLY | In a friendly, cordial manner |
| 7. | AMPOULE | Sealed glass or plastic bulb containing solutions for hypodermic injection |
| 8. | ANGULARITIES | Sharp corners; angular outlines |
| 9. | ASPHYXIATION | Death by choking, smothering, or suffocating |
| 10. | AUTOMATON | Mechanical figure; robot |
| 11. | AVERSION | Strong feeling of dislike, opposition, or repugnance |
| 12. | BARRICADED | Blocked with a defensive barrier |
| 13. | CAIRNGORM | Smoky-yellow to dark brown or black variety of quartz, used as a gem stone |
| 14. | CHANCERY | Division of the High Court of Justice of Great Britain |
| 15. | CLAMBERED | Climbed with difficulty, especially on all fours |
| 16. | CONCLAVE | Private or secret meeting |
| 17. | CONCURRED | Was of the same opinion; agreed |
| 18. | CONJURING | Affecting or influencing as if by invocation or a magic spell |
| 19. | COUNTENANCE | Look or expression of the face |
| 20. | COVERTLY | Secretly; in a concealed manner |
| 21. | CRYPTIC | Mysterious in meaning; puzzling; ambiguous |
| 22. | DEFERENTIAL | Showing regard or respect |
| 23. | DEPORTMENT | Demeanor; conduct; behavior |
| 24. | DESULTORY | Lacking in consistency or visible order; disconnected |
| 25. | DOGGEREL | Crudely or irregularly fashioned verse, often of a humorous or burlesque nature |
| 26. | DRAUGHT | Dose of liquid medicine |
| 27. | DUBIOUSLY | In a doubtful manner |
| 28. | EBONITE | Hard, non-resilient rubber formed by vulcanizing natural rubber |
| 29. | EJACULATIONS | Sudden, short exclamations, especially brief pious utterances or prayers |
| 30. | EXIGENCIES | Pressing or urgent situations |
| 31. | FEASIBLE | Capable of being done, effected, or accomplished |
| 32. | FRAUGHT | Filled or laden (with) |
| 33. | GIDDINESS | Dizziness |
| 34. | GIMLET | Small tool for boring holes |
| 35. | HELIOGRAPHING | Transmitting messages by reflecting sunlight |
| 36. | HITHERTO | Up to this time; until now |
| 37. | IMPROMPTU | Made or done without previous preparation |
| 38. | INCLINATION | Disposition or bent, esp. of the mind or will; a liking or preference |
| 39. | INDICTMENTS | Written statements charging a party with the commission of a crime |
| 40. | INERT | Unable to move or act |
| 41. | INEVITABILITY | Unable to be avoided, evaded, or escaped |
| 42. | INNOCUOUS | Harmless |
| 43. | INQUEST | Investigation made by a coroner into the cause of a death |
| 44. | INTERVAL | In between period of time |
| 45. | JETTY | Wharf; landing pier |
| 46. | LARDER | Room or place where food is stored; pantry |
| 47. | LASSITUDE | Weariness of body or mind from strain; lack of energy |

# And Then There Were None Vocabulary Word List Cont.

| No. | Word | Clue/Definition |
|---|---|---|
| 48. | LEGACY | Gift of property or money through a will; a bequest |
| 49. | MACKINTOSH | Raincoat |
| 50. | MALEVOLENTLY | In an evil, harmful, or injurious manner |
| 51. | MALICIOUS | Deliberately harmful or spiteful |
| 52. | OBLIQUELY | Having a slanting or sloping direction, course, or position |
| 53. | OBLIVION | State of being completely forgotten or unknown |
| 54. | OILSILK | Heavy, water-resistant fabric |
| 55. | PACIFICALLY | Peaceably, mildly, calmly, or quietly |
| 56. | PALL | Anything that covers, shrouds, or overspreads, esp. with darkness or gloom |
| 57. | PALPABLY | Plainly seen, heard, or perceived; obviously |
| 58. | PERITONITIS | Inflammation of the membrane surrounding the abdominal cavity |
| 59. | PETROL | Gasoline |
| 60. | PHYSIQUE | Physical or bodily structure; appearance |
| 61. | PIOUS | Characterized by a hypocritical concern with virtue or religious devotion |
| 62. | PRETENCE | False showing |
| 63. | PROBATIONER | Nurse in training who is undergoing a trial period |
| 64. | PROVISIONED | Provided a stock of necessary supplies, especially food |
| 65. | QUIETUS | Discharge or release from life |
| 66. | RECOILED | Shrunk back, as in fear or repugnance |
| 67. | RECONNAISSANCE | Search made for useful military information in the field |
| 68. | RECRIMINATION | Act of accusing in return |
| 69. | REPROACH | Find fault with; blame; censure |
| 70. | RIND | Thick and firm outer coat or covering |
| 71. | RUMINATING | Reflecting on over and over again; turning a matter over in the mind |
| 72. | SAGACITY | Acuteness of mental discernment and soundness of judgment |
| 73. | SERENELY | In a calm, peaceful, or tranquil manner |
| 74. | SIDEBOARD | Piece of dining room furniture having drawers and shelves for linens and tableware |
| 75. | SIPHON | Pipe or tube to draw off or convey liquid |
| 76. | SKEINS | Lengths of thread or yarn wound in loose, long coils |
| 77. | SOLICITUDE | Attitude expressing excessive attentiveness |
| 78. | STAMINA | Physical or moral strength to resist or withstand illness, fatigue, or hardship; endurance |
| 79. | STILETTO | A small dagger with a slender, tapering blade |
| 80. | STUPENDOUS | Causing amazement; astounding; marvelous |
| 81. | SUBSEQUENT | Occurring or coming later or after |
| 82. | SUFFUSED | Spread through or over, as with liquid, color, or light |
| 83. | SUPERLATIVELY | Of the highest kind, quality, or order; surpassing all else or others |
| 84. | SURREPTITIOUS | Taking pains to avoid being observed; cautious; stealthy |
| 85. | TENACIOUS | Holding fast; characterized by keeping a firm hold |
| 86. | UNHEEDED | Disregarded; ignored |
| 87. | UNOBTRUSIVELY | In a manner that is not undesirably noticeable or blatant |
| 88. | UNTENANTED | Unoccupied; not leased to or occupied by a tenant |
| 89. | VENTURE | Undertaking involving uncertainty as to the outcome |
| 90. | VERISIMILITUDE | Appearance or semblance of truth; likelihood; probability |

# And Then There Were None Vocabulary Word Search

```
C R E P R O A C H S U R R E P T I T I O U S S N
P O A M E W I U V F Q K R W R H M I V I A K O T
C F N M A T L E T I N O B E O G P N E N B L L D
A H W C P L R E C O I L E D V U R Q N C H V I N
V N A Y L O I O G P M J V F I A O U T L O E C W
E D R N A A U C L A A A G D S R M E U I R R I Y
R C E D C F V L I S C L T N I F P S R N R I T T
S L G S E E F E E O U Y L O O F T T E A E S U L
I A S V U P R A B C U F X W N I U C M T N I D F
O M W S T L O Y B K O S F B E Q L M V I T M E Y
N B D N N C T R H L L N F U D M S S S O C I D K
S E L O E Z O O T Z Y Y J L S E P T I N Q L A B
E R S I U T T N R M Q L N U I E A E R L T I C Y
D E U T Q T B N C Y E E N C R M D L Y D K T I K
U D T A E U D B T U S N N T I I N M W T T U R T
T M E L S Y E T M N R E T N C O N I H H D D R L
I Y I U B H E L I O G R A P H I N G S N O E A S
S T U C U J R E Y I Z E E P P F U U I G N R B C
S S Q A S M K W X H D S I D Q A O R D I D Z W S
A P H J S S Q E K Y J S K T R I I N T E R V A L
L V S E P A L P A B L Y S D P T C A R T S B A B
```

| | | | |
|---|---|---|---|
| ABHORRENT | DEPORTMENT | JETTY | REPROACH |
| ABSTRACT | DESULTORY | LARDER | RIND |
| AEONS | DRAUGHT | LASSITUDE | SERENELY |
| AFFABLY | EBONITE | LEGACY | SIPHON |
| AMPOULE | EJACULATIONS | MALICIOUS | SKEINS |
| AUTOMATON | EXIGENCIES | OBLIQUELY | SOLICITUDE |
| AVERSION | FRAUGHT | OILSILK | STAMINA |
| BARRICADED | GIMLET | PALL | STILETTO |
| CHANCERY | HELIOGRAPHING | PALPABLY | SUBSEQUENT |
| CLAMBERED | IMPROMPTU | PETROL | SUFFUSED |
| CONCLAVE | INCLINATION | PIOUS | SURREPTITIOUS |
| CONCURRED | INERT | PROVISIONED | VENTURE |
| CONJURING | INQUEST | QUIETUS | VERISIMILITUDE |
| CRYPTIC | INTERVAL | RECOILED | |

# And Then There Were None Vocabulary Word Search Answer Key

```
C R E P R O A C H S U R R E P T I T I O U S S
  O A M E   I U         R H M I V I A   O
C   N M A T L E T I N O B E O G P N E N B   L
A H   C P L R E C O I L E D V U R Q N C H V I
V   A Y L O I   O G P M     I A O U T L O E C
E   D R N A A U C L A A A   S R M E U I R R I
R C E D C F V L I S C L T   I F P S R N R I T
S L   S E E F E E O U Y L O O   T T E A E S U
I A     U P R A   C U F   N I U   T N I D
O M   S T L O Y B   O S F   E L   I T M E
N B   N N C T R   L   N   U   S S O   I D
  E L O E   O O T   Y Y J   S E   T I N   L A
E R S I   U   T N R M   L   U I E A E   L I C
D E U T Q T     C Y E E   C R M D L   K T I
U D T A E U       T U S N N   I I N M   T U R T
T   E L S     E T   N R E T N   O N I H D D R L
I   I U B H E L I O G R A P H I N G S N O E A
S T U C U J   E Y I     E E P   U U I   N R B
S   Q A S   K   X     S I D   A O R   I D
A   J     S   E         R I N T E R V A L
L     E P A L P A B L Y   D P T C A R T S B A
```

| ABHORRENT | DEPORTMENT | JETTY | REPROACH |
| ABSTRACT | DESULTORY | LARDER | RIND |
| AEONS | DRAUGHT | LASSITUDE | SERENELY |
| AFFABLY | EBONITE | LEGACY | SIPHON |
| AMPOULE | EJACULATIONS | MALICIOUS | SKEINS |
| AUTOMATON | EXIGENCIES | OBLIQUELY | SOLICITUDE |
| AVERSION | FRAUGHT | OILSILK | STAMINA |
| BARRICADED | GIMLET | PALL | STILETTO |
| CHANCERY | HELIOGRAPHING | PALPABLY | SUBSEQUENT |
| CLAMBERED | IMPROMPTU | PETROL | SUFFUSED |
| CONCLAVE | INCLINATION | PIOUS | SURREPTITIOUS |
| CONCURRED | INERT | PROVISIONED | VENTURE |
| CONJURING | INQUEST | QUIETUS | VERISIMILITUDE |
| CRYPTIC | INTERVAL | RECOILED | |

# And Then There Were None Vocabulary Crossword

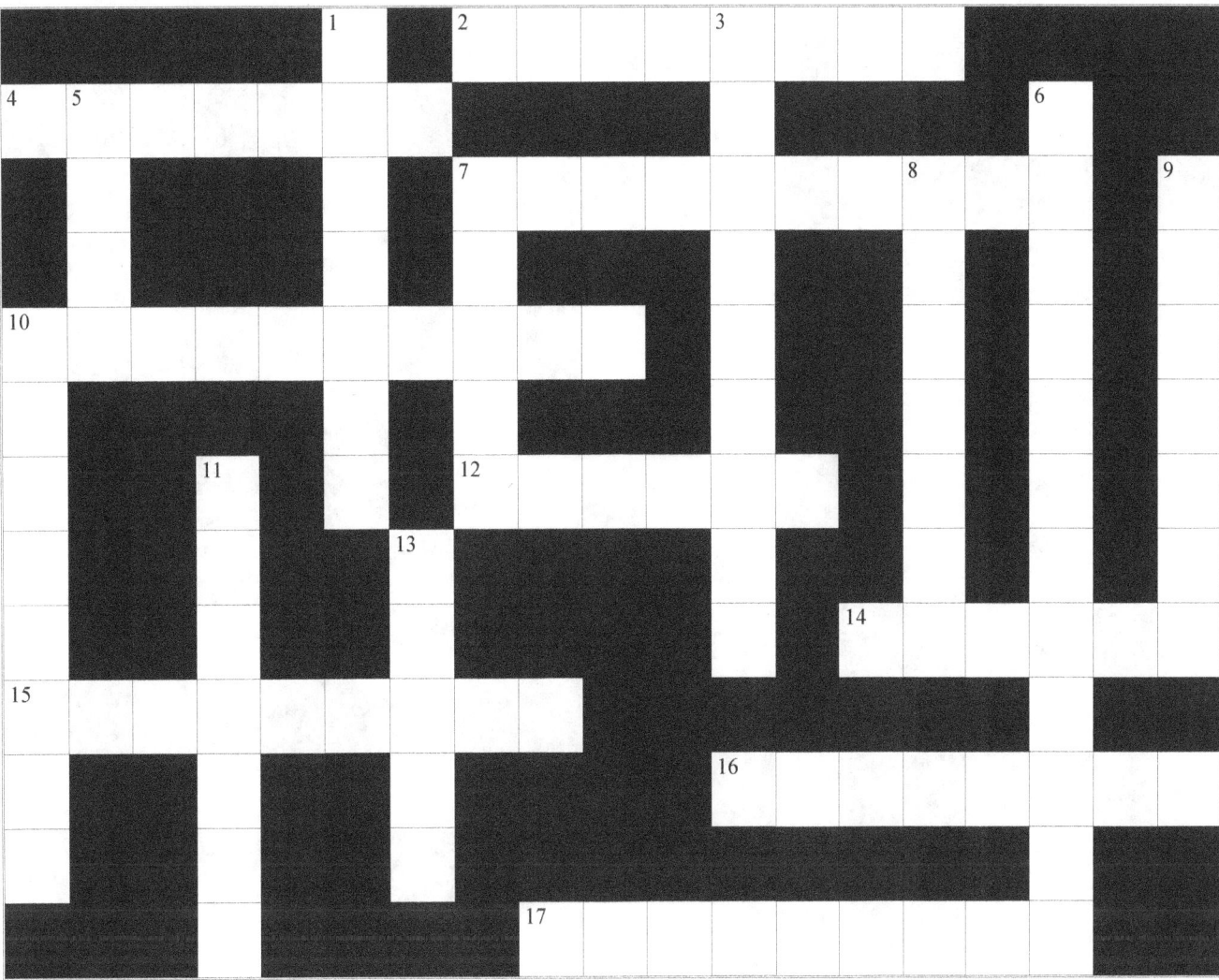

Across
2. Division of the High Court of Justice of Great Britain
4. Mysterious in meaning; puzzling; ambiguous
7. Expertise or nimbleness in the use of the hands or body
10. Serving to warn, especially to correct
12. Pipe or tube to draw off or convey liquid
14. Gift of property or money through a will; a bequest
15. Detestable; loathsome; hateful
16. Strong feeling of dislike, opposition, or repugnance
17. Mechanical figure; robot

Down
1. Heavy, water-resistant fabric
3. Smoky-yellow to dark brown or black variety of quartz, used as a gem stone
5. Thick and firm outer coat or covering
6. Death by choking, smothering, or suffocating
7. Indefinitely long periods of time
8. Hard, non-resilient rubber formed by vulcanizing natural rubber
9. In a friendly, cordial manner
10. Theoretical; not applied or practical
11. Sealed glass or plastic bulb containing solutions for hypodermic injection
13. Unable to move or act

# And Then There Were None Vocabulary Crossword Answer Key

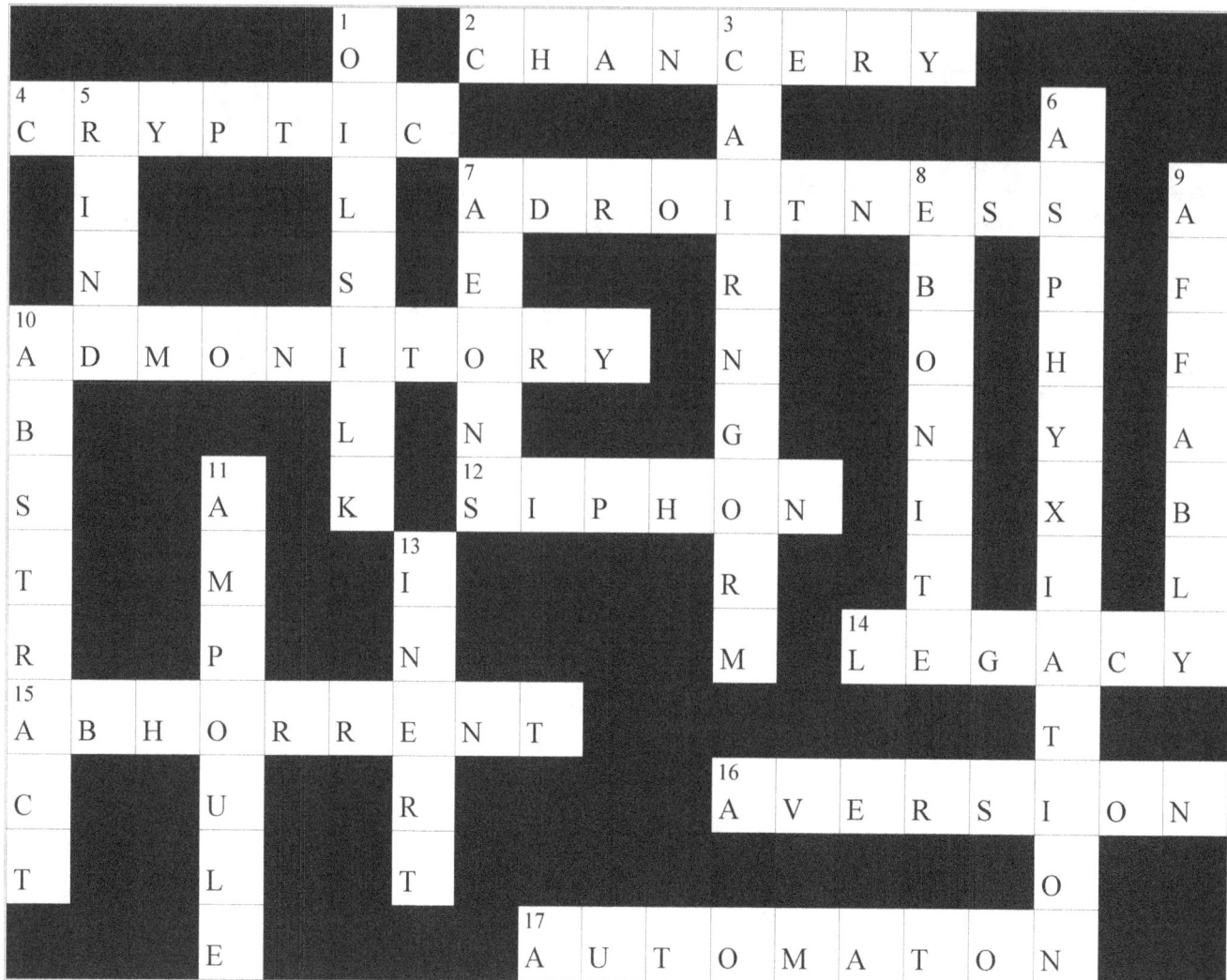

Across
2. Division of the High Court of Justice of Great Britain
4. Mysterious in meaning; puzzling; ambiguous
7. Expertise or nimbleness in the use of the hands or body
10. Serving to warn, especially to correct
12. Pipe or tube to draw off or convey liquid
14. Gift of property or money through a will; a bequest
15. Detestable; loathsome; hateful
16. Strong feeling of dislike, opposition, or repugnance
17. Mechanical figure; robot

Down
1. Heavy, water-resistant fabric
3. Smoky-yellow to dark brown or black variety of quartz, used as a gem stone
5. Thick and firm outer coat or covering
6. Death by choking, smothering, or suffocating
7. Indefinitely long periods of time
8. Hard, non-resilient rubber formed by vulcanizing natural rubber
9. In a friendly, cordial manner
10. Theoretical; not applied or practical
11. Sealed glass or plastic bulb containing solutions for hypodermic injection
13. Unable to move or act

And Then There Were None Vocabulary Matching 1

___ 1. FEASIBLE	A. Dizziness
___ 2. BARRICADED	B. Hard, non-resilient rubber formed by vulcanizing natural rubber
___ 3. AVERSION	C. Sharp corners; angular outlines
___ 4. SUBSEQUENT	D. Shrunk back, as in fear or repugnance
___ 5. QUIETUS	E. In between period of time
___ 6. CONCURRED	F. Acuteness of mental discernment and soundness of judgment
___ 7. UNOBTRUSIVELY	G. Indefinitely long periods of time
___ 8. INEVITABILITY	H. Blocked with a defensive barrier
___ 9. INCLINATION	I. Small tool for boring holes
___10. GIMLET	J. Having a slanting or sloping direction, course, or position
___11. OBLIQUELY	K. Disposition or bent, esp. of the mind or will; a liking or preference
___12. HELIOGRAPHING	L. Transmitting messages by reflecting sunlight
___13. CONJURING	M. Detestable; loathsome; hateful
___14. INTERVAL	N. Smoky-yellow to dark brown or black variety of quartz, used as a gem stone
___15. AEONS	O. Affecting or influencing as if by invocation or a magic spell
___16. ABHORRENT	P. Crudely or irregularly fashioned verse, often of a humorous or burlesque nature
___17. GIDDINESS	Q. Occurring or coming later or after
___18. ANGULARITIES	R. Capable of being done, effected, or accomplished
___19. SIPHON	S. Discharge or release from life
___20. INERT	T. Strong feeling of dislike, opposition, or repugnance
___21. RECOILED	U. Was of the same opinion; agreed
___22. EBONITE	V. Pipe or tube to draw off or convey liquid
___23. DOGGEREL	W. In a manner that is not undesirably noticeable or blatant
___24. SAGACITY	X. Unable to move or act
___25. CAIRNGORM	Y. Unable to be avoided, evaded, or escaped

## And Then There Were None Vocabulary Matching 1 Answer Key

R - 1. FEASIBLE     A. Dizziness

H - 2. BARRICADED     B. Hard, non-resilient rubber formed by vulcanizing natural rubber

T - 3. AVERSION     C. Sharp corners; angular outlines

Q - 4. SUBSEQUENT     D. Shrunk back, as in fear or repugnance

S - 5. QUIETUS     E. In between period of time

U - 6. CONCURRED     F. Acuteness of mental discernment and soundness of judgment

W - 7. UNOBTRUSIVELY     G. Indefinitely long periods of time

Y - 8. INEVITABILITY     H. Blocked with a defensive barrier

K - 9. INCLINATION     I. Small tool for boring holes

I - 10. GIMLET     J. Having a slanting or sloping direction, course, or position

J - 11. OBLIQUELY     K. Disposition or bent, esp. of the mind or will; a liking or preference

L - 12. HELIOGRAPHING     L. Transmitting messages by reflecting sunlight

O - 13. CONJURING     M. Detestable; loathsome; hateful

E - 14. INTERVAL     N. Smoky-yellow to dark brown or black variety of quartz, used as a gem stone

G - 15. AEONS     O. Affecting or influencing as if by invocation or a magic spell

M - 16. ABHORRENT     P. Crudely or irregularly fashioned verse, often of a humorous or burlesque nature

A - 17. GIDDINESS     Q. Occurring or coming later or after

C - 18. ANGULARITIES     R. Capable of being done, effected, or accomplished

V - 19. SIPHON     S. Discharge or release from life

X - 20. INERT     T. Strong feeling of dislike, opposition, or repugnance

D - 21. RECOILED     U. Was of the same opinion; agreed

B - 22. EBONITE     V. Pipe or tube to draw off or convey liquid

P - 23. DOGGEREL     W. In a manner that is not undesirably noticeable or blatant

F - 24. SAGACITY     X. Unable to move or act

N - 25. CAIRNGORM     Y. Unable to be avoided, evaded, or escaped

# And Then There Were None Vocabulary Matching 2

___ 1. DUBIOUSLY
___ 2. RUMINATING
___ 3. SUPERLATIVELY
___ 4. CHANCERY
___ 5. DEFERENTIAL
___ 6. INEVITABILITY
___ 7. REPROACH
___ 8. HITHERTO
___ 9. SUFFUSED
___ 10. RECONNAISSANCE
___ 11. UNOBTRUSIVELY
___ 12. ADMONITORY
___ 13. ABHORRENT
___ 14. AFFABLY
___ 15. MACKINTOSH
___ 16. PACIFICALLY
___ 17. STAMINA
___ 18. UNHEEDED
___ 19. RIND
___ 20. FEASIBLE
___ 21. VERISIMILITUDE
___ 22. OBLIQUELY
___ 23. SUBSEQUENT
___ 24. EJACULATIONS
___ 25. PALPABLY

A. Showing regard or respect
B. In a manner that is not undesirably noticeable or blatant
C. Up to this time; until now
D. In a doubtful manner
E. Having a slanting or sloping direction, course, or position
F. Plainly seen, heard, or perceived; obviously
G. Search made for useful military information in the field
H. Appearance or semblance of truth; likelihood; probability
I. Spread through or over, as with liquid, color, or light
J. Thick and firm outer coat or covering
K. Raincoat
L. Peaceably, mildly, calmly, or quietly
M. Reflecting on over and over again; turning a matter over in the mind
N. Serving to warn, especially to correct
O. Unable to be avoided, evaded, or escaped
P. Find fault with; blame; censure
Q. Capable of being done, effected, or accomplished
R. Sudden, short exclamations, especially brief pious utterances or prayers
S. Disregarded; ignored
T. Detestable; loathsome; hateful
U. Occurring or coming later or after
V. Division of the High Court of Justice of Great Britain
W. Physical or moral strength to resist or withstand illness, fatigue, or hardship; endurance
X. Of the highest kind, quality, or order; surpassing all else or others
Y. In a friendly, cordial manner

# And Then There Were None Vocabulary Matching 2 Answer Key

| | | |
|---|---|---|
| D - 1. DUBIOUSLY | A. | Showing regard or respect |
| M - 2. RUMINATING | B. | In a manner that is not undesirably noticeable or blatant |
| X - 3. SUPERLATIVELY | C. | Up to this time; until now |
| V - 4. CHANCERY | D. | In a doubtful manner |
| A - 5. DEFERENTIAL | E. | Having a slanting or sloping direction, course, or position |
| O - 6. INEVITABILITY | F. | Plainly seen, heard, or perceived; obviously |
| P - 7. REPROACH | G. | Search made for useful military information in the field |
| C - 8. HITHERTO | H. | Appearance or semblance of truth; likelihood; probability |
| I - 9. SUFFUSED | I. | Spread through or over, as with liquid, color, or light |
| G -10. RECONNAISSANCE | J. | Thick and firm outer coat or covering |
| B -11. UNOBTRUSIVELY | K. | Raincoat |
| N -12. ADMONITORY | L. | Peaceably, mildly, calmly, or quietly |
| T -13. ABHORRENT | M. | Reflecting on over and over again; turning a matter over in the mind |
| Y -14. AFFABLY | N. | Serving to warn, especially to correct |
| K -15. MACKINTOSH | O. | Unable to be avoided, evaded, or escaped |
| L -16. PACIFICALLY | P. | Find fault with; blame; censure |
| W  17. STAMINA | Q. | Capable of being done, effected, or accomplished |
| S -18. UNHEEDED | R. | Sudden, short exclamations, especially brief pious utterances or prayers |
| J - 19. RIND | S. | Disregarded; ignored |
| Q -20. FEASIBLE | T. | Detestable; loathsome; hateful |
| H -21. VERISIMILITUDE | U. | Occurring or coming later or after |
| E -22. OBLIQUELY | V. | Division of the High Court of Justice of Great Britain |
| U -23. SUBSEQUENT | W. | Physical or moral strength to resist or withstand illness, fatigue, or hardship; endurance |
| R -24. EJACULATIONS | X. | Of the highest kind, quality, or order; surpassing all else or others |
| F -25. PALPABLY | Y. | In a friendly, cordial manner |

## And Then There Were None Vocabulary Juggle Letters 1

1. SBAELFEI = 1. _____
   Capable of being done, effected, or accomplished

2. TMELGI = 2. _____
   Small tool for boring holes

3. NRTEI = 3. _____
   Unable to move or act

4. TRHDAUG = 4. _____
   Dose of liquid medicine

5. LEIICSUTOD = 5. _____
   Attitude expressing excessive attentiveness

6. NILIIOTACNN = 6. _____
   Disposition or bent, esp. of the mind or will; a liking or preference

7. LVTAESRILUYPE = 7. _____
   Of the highest kind, quality, or order; surpassing all else or others

8. IVDRPSINOEO = 8. _____
   Provided a stock of necessary supplies, especially food

9. NSEBESQTUU = 9. _____
   Occurring or coming later or after

10. ATPNBROIROE =10. _____
    Nurse in training who is undergoing a trial period

11. FAYALBF =11. _____
    In a friendly, cordial manner

12. TIIEEVDUSIIMRL =12. _____
    Appearance or semblance of truth; likelihood; probability

13. SONDSUPUTE =13. _____
    Causing amazement; astounding; marvelous

14. CUSONONUI =14. _____
    Harmless

# And Then There Were None Vocabulary Juggle Letters 1 Answer Key

1. SBAELFEI = 1. FEASIBLE
   Capable of being done, effected, or accomplished

2. TMELGI = 2. GIMLET
   Small tool for boring holes

3. NRTEI = 3. INERT
   Unable to move or act

4. TRHDAUG = 4. DRAUGHT
   Dose of liquid medicine

5. LEIICSUTOD = 5. SOLICITUDE
   Attitude expressing excessive attentiveness

6. NILIIOTACNN = 6. INCLINATION
   Disposition or bent, esp. of the mind or will; a liking or preference

7. LVTAESRILUYPE = 7. SUPERLATIVELY
   Of the highest kind, quality, or order; surpassing all else or others

8. IVDRPSINOEO = 8. PROVISIONED
   Provided a stock of necessary supplies, especially food

9. NSEBESQTUU = 9. SUBSEQUENT
   Occurring or coming later or after

10. ATPNBROIROE =10. PROBATIONER
    Nurse in training who is undergoing a trial period

11. FAYALBF =11. AFFABLY
    In a friendly, cordial manner

12. TIIEEVDUSIIMRL =12. VERISIMILITUDE
    Appearance or semblance of truth; likelihood; probability

13. SONDSUPUTE =13. STUPENDOUS
    Causing amazement; astounding; marvelous

14. CUSONONUI =14. INNOCUOUS
    Harmless

And Then There Were None Vocabulary Juggle Letters 2

1. IIERLSVITEDIMU = 1. _____
   Appearance or semblance of truth; likelihood; probability

2. TRONEPAIRBO = 2. _____
   Nurse in training who is undergoing a trial period

3. AGOMRRCNI = 3. _____
   Smoky-yellow to dark brown or black variety of quartz, used as a gem stone

4. NUOAMOTAT = 4. _____
   Mechanical figure; robot

5. OANPIYXITHSA = 5. _____
   Death by choking, smothering, or suffocating

6. OIOVNIBL = 6. _____
   State of being completely forgotten or unknown

7. ETTJY = 7. _____
   Wharf; landing pier

8. DNTNTNAEUE = 8. _____
   Unoccupied; not leased to or occupied by a tenant

9. BSQUUSETNE = 9. _____
   Occurring or coming later or after

10. GDLEGERO = 10. _____
    Crudely or irregularly fashioned verse, often of a humorous or burlesque nature

11. PRUMPOMIT = 11. _____
    Made or done without previous preparation

12. LOTTITES = 12. _____
    A small dagger with a slender, tapering blade

13. ENIATCSUO = 13. _____
    Holding fast; characterized by keeping a firm hold

14. IALENVTR = 14. _____
    In between period of time

## And Then There Were None Vocabulary Juggle Letters 2 Answer Key

1. IIERLSVITEDIMU = 1. VERISIMILITUDE
   Appearance or semblance of truth; likelihood; probability

2. TRONEPAIRBO = 2. PROBATIONER
   Nurse in training who is undergoing a trial period

3. AGOMRRCNI = 3. CAIRNGORM
   Smoky-yellow to dark brown or black variety of quartz, used as a gem stone

4. NUOAMOTAT = 4. AUTOMATON
   Mechanical figure; robot

5. OANPIYXITHSA = 5. ASPHYXIATION
   Death by choking, smothering, or suffocating

6. OIOVNIBL = 6. OBLIVION
   State of being completely forgotten or unknown

7. ETTJY = 7. JETTY
   Wharf; landing pier

8. DNTNTNAEUE = 8. UNTENANTED
   Unoccupied; not leased to or occupied by a tenant

9. BSQUUSETNE = 9. SUBSEQUENT
   Occurring or coming later or after

10. GDLEGERO =10. DOGGEREL
    Crudely or irregularly fashioned verse, often of a humorous or burlesque nature

11. PRUMPOMIT =11. IMPROMPTU
    Made or done without previous preparation

12. LOTTITES =12. STILETTO
    A small dagger with a slender, tapering blade

13. ENIATCSUO =13. TENACIOUS
    Holding fast; characterized by keeping a firm hold

14. IALENVTR =14. INTERVAL
    In between period of time